LEGAL AID, SENTENCING AND PUNISHMENT OF OFFENDERS ACT 2012

EXPLANATORY NOTES

INTRODUCTION

1. These Explanatory Notes relate to the Legal Aid, Sentencing and Punishment of Offenders Act 2012 which received Royal Assent on 1 May 2012. They have been prepared by the Ministry of Justice in order to assist the reader in their understanding of the Act. They do not form part of the Act and have not been endorsed by Parliament.

2. The Notes need to be read in conjunction with the Act. They are not, and are not meant to be, a comprehensive description of the Act. So where a section or part of a section does not seem to require any explanation or comment, none is given.

3. A table setting out the meaning of abbreviations used in the Notes is at Annex A.

BACKGROUND

4. The Legal Aid, Sentencing and Punishment of Offenders Act 2012 has 4 Parts and 27 Schedules.

Part 1: Legal aid

5. Part 1 of the Access to Justice Act 1999 sets out the current statutory framework for legal aid in England and Wales. That Act established the Legal Services Commission ("the LSC"), the non-departmental public body responsible for administering civil and criminal legal aid schemes in England and Wales. It also gives the Lord Chancellor powers to set the overall scope of legal aid, along with a number of powers and duties in relation to the LSC.

6. In *The Coalition: Our Programme for Government*, the Government set out its intention to "carry out a fundamental review of legal aid to make it work more efficiently."

7. In March 2010, Sir Ian Magee published the conclusions of his review into the delivery of legal aid. A key recommendation was that consideration should be given to transferring the administration of the civil and criminal legal aid schemes to an executive agency of the Ministry of Justice. The previous Government announced later that month that it had accepted this recommendation. In November 2010 the Ministry of Justice published a consultation paper on proposals for reform of legal aid (see paragraph 8 below). In the paper the coalition Government stated that it had

reached a similar conclusion and would seek to legislate when parliamentary time allowed. The Act therefore contains provisions to abolish the LSC and transfer the day-to-day administration of legal aid to the Lord Chancellor. In practice, this will be done by civil servants in an executive agency of the Ministry of Justice. However, decisions on legal aid in individual cases will be taken by a statutory office holder: a civil servant designated by the Lord Chancellor as the Director of Legal Aid Casework. The Lord Chancellor will have no power to direct or issue guidance to the Director in relation to individual cases.

8. The Ministry of Justice published a consultation paper entitled *"Proposals for the Reform of Legal Aid in England and Wales"*[1] on 15 November 2010. The consultation closed on 14 February 2011. On 21 June 2011 the Government published its response to the consultation, which set out its finalised proposals for reform[2]. This Act implements many of these proposals.

Part 2: Litigation funding and costs

9. The Ministry of Justice published on 15 November 2010 a further consultation paper entitled *"Proposals for reform of civil litigation funding and costs in England and Wales"*[3] which relates to proposals from Lord Justice Jackson's review[4] (published in January 2010). This consultation exercise closed on 14 February 2011. On 29 March 2011 the Government published its response to the consultation exercise, announcing its intention to implement the proposals to reform "no win no fee" conditional fee agreements ("CFAs")[5]. This Act implements those proposals.

10. On 9 September 2011, the Government announced its intention to ban referral fees in personal injury claims via written ministerial statement to Parliament[6] as part of the wider package of reforms of civil litigation funding and costs. Provision to achieve that is now made in Part 2 of the Act.

11. In some circumstances, the courts have power to order that an amount in respect of costs incurred by a successful defendant, witness or successful appellant is to be paid out of central funds (in other words, out of money provided by Parliament). In the case of *R (on the application of the Law Society of England and Wales) v Lord Chancellor*[7] in June 2010, the court held that the Lord Chancellor cannot cap the

---

[1] *"Proposals for the Reform of Legal Aid in England and Wales"* Cm 7967 available at:
http://www.justice.gov.uk/consultations/legal-aid-reform-151110.htm
[2] The Government's response is available at: http://www.justice.gov.uk. It is Command Paper CM8072.
[3] *"Proposals for reform of civil litigation funding and costs in England and Wales"* Cm 7947 available at
http://www.justice.gov.uk/consultations/jackson-review-151110.htm
[4] Ministry of Justice (2010) *"Review of Civil Litigation Costs: Final Report"*. Norwich, TSO available at
http://www.judiciary.gov.uk/publications-and-reports/reports/civil/review-of-civil-litigation-costs/civil-litigation-costs-review-reports
[5] *"Reforming Civil Litigation Funding and Costs in England and Wales – Implementation of Lord Justice Jackson's Recommendations: The Government Response"* Cm 8041 available at
http://www.justice.gov.uk/consultations/566.htm
[6] *Personal Injury Cases (referral fees)*, available at:
http://www.publications.parliament.uk/pa/cm201011/cmhansrd/cm110909/wmstext/110909m0001.htm#110909
87000046
[7] *R (on the application of the Law Society of England and Wales) v Lord Chancellor* available at
www.bailii.org/ew/cases/EWHC/Admin/2010/1406.html

amounts that the courts award. This Act will provide the Lord Chancellor with a power to do so for the purposes of proceedings in England and Wales, other than in relation to costs incurred in proceedings in the Supreme Court. It will also largely prevent orders being made in respect of legal costs (that is, lawyers' fees, charges and disbursements including expert witness costs) where legal aid is available.

Part 3 Sentencing and Punishment of Offenders

12.   The current sentencing framework is broadly governed by the Criminal Justice Act 2003 ("the 2003 Act").

13.   In *The Coalition: Our Programme for Government*, the Government set out its intention to: *"conduct a full review of sentencing policy to ensure that it is effective in deterring crime, protecting the public, punishing offenders and cutting reoffending."*

14.   On 7 December 2010, the Ministry of Justice published a consultation paper entitled *"Breaking the Cycle: Effective Punishment, Rehabilitation and Sentencing of Offenders"*[8]. The document set out the Government's plans to cut crime and reoffending through fundamental changes to the criminal justice system. The consultation paper proposed a number of reforms to the existing sentencing legislation including a number of changes to the sentencing framework, reform of release and recall arrangements, and reforms to the youth justice system. The consultation ran for 12 weeks and concluded on 4 March 2011. The Ministry of Justice published its response to the consultation on 21 June 2011. This Act implements a number of the sentencing reforms that formed part of the consultation.

15.   On 13 July 2011, the Ministry of Justice published a consultation paper entitled *"Options for dealing with squatting."*[9] The purpose of the consultation was to gather more information about the nature and extent of squatting in England and Wales, and to invite views on whether, and how, existing criminal and civil mechanisms should be strengthened to deal with it. The consultation ran for 12 weeks and concluded on 5 October 2011. The Ministry of Justice published its response to the consultation on 26 October 2011. Following the consultation, a new offence of squatting in a residential building was added to the Bill during its passage through Parliament (see what is now section 144).

---

[8] *"Breaking the Cycle: Effective Punishment, Rehabilitation and Sentencing of Offenders"* Cm 7972 available at www.justice.gov.uk/consultations/consultation-040311
[9] *"Options for dealing with squatting"* CP12/2011 available at www.justice.gov.uk/consultations/dealing-with-squatters.htm.

SUMMARY

16.   A summary of the Act is set out below:

Part 1: Legal Aid

17.   Part 1 of the Act abolishes the LSC and places a duty on the Lord Chancellor, subject to the provisions of Part 1, to secure the availability of civil and criminal legal aid. The intention is that an executive agency within the Ministry of Justice will administer the delivery of legal aid services in England and Wales. However, in relation to decision-making in individual cases, the Act requires the Lord Chancellor to designate a civil servant to be the Director of Legal Aid Casework ("the Director"). The Director will have statutory responsibility for taking decisions on legal aid in individual cases. The Act prevents the Lord Chancellor from giving directions or guidance to the Director in relation to individual cases.

18.   Provisions in Part 1 ensure that, together with the powers the Lord Chancellor has as a Minister of the Crown, the Lord Chancellor has power to enter into appropriate arrangements with others for them to provide legal aid. The Lord Chancellor will have power to set quality standards for those providing legal aid services and to make arrangements for accreditation and monitoring of such providers. (the LSC currently have accreditation schemes such as the Specialist Quality Mark, responsibility for which will fall to the Lord Chancellor once the LSC is abolished). The Lord Chancellor will have power to make provision in regulations about the payment of remuneration to those providing legal aid services.

Civil legal aid

19.   Part 1 of the Act defines civil legal services as encompassing advice, assistance and representation by legal professionals and also the services of non-legal professionals, including for example mediation and other forms of dispute resolution.

20.   Part 1 of Schedule 1 describes the civil legal services that can generally be made available under the arrangements for civil legal aid.

21.   The Act also provides the Director with the power to require civil legal services not mentioned in Schedule 1 to be made available, *either* where the Director considers that it is necessary to make the services available because the failure to provide legal services to an individual would be a breach of the individual's Convention rights (within the meaning of the Human Rights Act 1998), or any rights of the individual to the provision of legal services that are enforceable EU rights, *or* where the Director considers that it is appropriate to make services available, in the particular circumstances of the case, having regard to any risk that failure to do so would result in a breach of such rights.

22.   The Act requires the Director to determine whether an individual qualifies for civil legal services by reference to their financial resources and the criteria set out in regulations prepared by the Lord Chancellor. The Act lists the factors which the Lord Chancellor must consider in setting those criteria. They are similar to the factors that

the LSC is currently required to consider when setting the Funding Code criteria (see section 8(2) of the Access to Justice Act 1999).

23.   The Act also provides the Lord Chancellor with a power to make regulations about the making and withdrawal of determinations by the Director about civil legal aid, including regulations about the means by which an application for legal aid must be made. The regulations must make provision about the review of determinations and may make provision about appeals against determinations.

Criminal legal aid

24.   Part 1 of the Act makes provision for individuals in custody at a police station or facing criminal investigation to be able to secure the provision of advice and assistance, including advocacy (usually by a duty solicitor). Determinations about whether individuals qualify for such services must be made having regard, in particular, to the interests of justice.

25.   The Act also provides for individuals to be provided with representation for criminal proceedings. Whether such services should be provided is to be determined having regard to the interests of justice and, where provided for in regulations, following an assessment of the individual's financial resources. Determinations about whether an individual qualifies for criminal legal aid will be made by the Director or by a court. Provisional determinations may be made in favour of individuals involved in a criminal investigation. Such a determination may be made, for example, where plea negotiations are initiated by a prosecutor under the guidelines issued by the Attorney General.

Contributions and costs

26.   Part 1 of the Act makes provision about determining the financial eligibility of individuals for civil and criminal legal aid. It also makes provision about when individuals can be required to make payments in connection with the provision of civil or criminal legal aid and about the enforcement of such requirements. The Act provides for a statutory charge over property that a legally aided person recovers or preserves, or over costs payable to them, in civil proceedings and the settlement of civil disputes. It also makes provision about costs in civil proceedings, including limiting the costs that can be awarded against a person receiving civil legal aid to the amount (if any) that is reasonable, given the financial resources of both parties and their conduct during the case.

Providers of services

27.   Part 1 of the Act enables the Lord Chancellor to restrict the choice of provider in certain conditions, for example to providers who hold a contract with the Lord Chancellor to provide such services. In publicly funded cases the professional relationship between provider and client is unaffected. The Act restricts payments to providers of legal aid from other sources and enables regulations to provide that, where legal aid is withdrawn, the provider is still to be paid for work undertaken.

28.   The Act provides for a code of conduct for any civil servants, or employees of a body established by the Lord Chancellor, who provide legal aid services. The code is to be published and laid before Parliament.

Part 2: Litigation funding and costs

29.   Part 2 of the Act contains provisions to implement reforms to the existing arrangements for civil litigation funding and costs as recommended by Lord Justice Jackson, a judge of the Court of Appeal, in his *Review of Civil Litigation Costs: Final Report.*[10]

30.   This Part of the Act also amends the Matrimonial Causes Act 1973 and the Civil Partnership Act 2004 to give the court powers to make orders in divorce proceedings, and corresponding civil partnership proceedings, for payments to be made by one party to another for the purposes of paying for legal services.

31.   Part 2 of the Act provides for the prohibition in personal injury cases both of the payment of referral fees (for access to potential claimants) by regulated persons, such as solicitors, to third parties, such as claims management companies and insurers, and of the receipt of such fees. Provision is also made for a power to extend the prohibition to other types of claim and legal services. It will be for the appropriate regulators, for example the Law Society, the Claims Management Regulator and the Financial Services Authority, to enforce the prohibition.

32.   In Part 2 of the Act, section 61 amends the Legal Services Act 2007 to enable the Supreme Court to make costs orders in civil proceedings where a successful party is represented pro bono, with the monies recovered going to a prescribed charity.

33.   Part 2 of the Act also amends the Prosecution of Offences Act 1985 ("POA 1985") by restricting the powers of the courts in England and Wales to order the payment out of central funds of amounts in respect of costs incurred by defendants, witnesses and appellants in criminal proceedings, particularly amounts in respect of legal costs (that is, lawyers' fees, charges and disbursements including expert witness costs). Similar restrictions are to be applied to amounts awarded by courts in respect of costs incurred by persons who make representations to a court in England and Wales in the course of references made by the Attorney General, persons who are discharged following extradition proceedings in England and Wales and persons involved in proceedings before the Court Martial Appeals Court. The restrictions will not apply in relation to costs incurred in proceedings in the Supreme Court.

Part 3: Sentencing and punishment of offenders
Chapter 1: Sentencing

34.   Chapter 1 sets out changes to some general sentencing provisions contained in the 2003 Act and other legislation. In particular it does the following:

- It imposes a duty on courts to consider the imposition of compensation orders for certain types of offence;

---

[10] Ministry of Justice (2010) *"Review of Civil Litigation Costs: Final Report"*, available at
http://www.judiciary.gov.uk/publications-and-reports/reports/civil/review-of-civil-litigation-costs/civil-litigation-costs-review-reports

- It simplifies the provision setting out the court's duty to give reasons for and to explain the effect of a sentence imposed by the court;

- It adds transgender identity to the personal characteristics which will be statutory aggravating factors in sentencing where any offence is motivated by hostility to the victim on this basis. It also provides for a starting point of 30 years for the minimum term for a life sentence for murder aggravated on the grounds of the victim's disability or transgender identity;

- It makes a number of changes in relation to community orders for adults. These are non-custodial sentences with specific treatment or behaviour requirements attached. It clarifies when community orders come to an end and enables a court to impose a fine for breach of a community order. It makes amendments to certain requirements that may be imposed as part of community orders and suspended sentence orders, in particular curfew requirements and mental health, drug rehabilitation and alcohol treatment requirements. It also creates new powers to prohibit foreign travel and to impose alcohol abstinence and monitoring requirements as part of an order.

- It amends the court's power to suspend a prison sentence by increasing the length of sentences that can be suspended, giving the court discretion not to impose community requirements as part of the sentence and enabling it to impose a fine for breach of a suspended sentence order.

- It provides for offences currently punishable by the magistrates' court on summary conviction with a maximum fine of £5,000 to be punishable by an unlimited fine instead and gives the Secretary of State power to increase the maximum sentences of certain other fines and the sums specified as levels 1- 4 on the standard scale of fines.

35. Chapter 1 amends the sentencing provisions of the Powers of Criminal Courts (Sentencing) Act 2000 that apply to youths. These will enable a court to impose a penalty for breach of a detention and training order even where the order has finished its term. The Chapter amends provisions about referral orders to provide more flexibility and discretion for their repeated use. It also applies a number of the changes made in relation to community orders to youth rehabilitation orders.

36. Chapter 1 repeals an unimplemented provision in the 2003 Act relating to "custody plus", which was a new type of sentence for offenders sentenced to less than 12 months imprisonment, and intermittent custody, which would have enabled offenders to spend part of their sentence in prison and part in the community.

Chapter 2: Bail
37. Chapter 2 makes a number of changes (contained in Schedule 11) to restrict the court's powers to remand adult unconvicted defendants in custody where it is apparent that there is no real prospect that the defendant would receive a custodial sentence if convicted. A court would still be able to remand in custody for the defendant's own protection, or where there was a risk of further offending involving domestic violence.

38.   A similar restriction on the remand to youth detention accommodation of defendants under 18 is made by Chapter 3 of Part 3 of the Act.

39.   The definition of 'young person' in the Bail Act 1976 is amended to include 17 year olds. This amendment is made as a consequence of changes to the provisions about remands for youths, the provisions for which are set out in Chapter 3 of Part 3 of the Act.

40.   In addition, the Bail (Amendment) Act 1993 is amended so that the prosecution may appeal to the High Court against the decision of the judge of a Crown Court to grant bail to a person charged with or convicted of an imprisonable offence.

Chapter 3: Remand of children otherwise than on bail

41.   Chapter 3 creates new custodial remand provisions for under 18s who are charged with or convicted of a criminal offence or concerned in extradition proceedings. It repeals the existing framework set out in the Children and Young Persons Act 1969 and removes provisions under which 17 year olds are currently remanded in prison.

42.   This Chapter makes provision for all under 18s who have been refused bail to be remanded in custody according to the same tests. It removes the existing distinctions based on age and gender and imposes a more rigorous test before under 18s can be remanded to youth detention accommodation.

Chapter 4: Release on licence etc.

43.   Chapter 4 makes amendments to the 2003 Act provisions about the release and recall of prisoners. As amended by this Chapter, the 2003 Act will apply to all sentences to be imposed for offences whenever they were committed and whenever the sentence was passed. Schedules 16 and 17 insert Schedules 20A and 20B into the 2003 Act and save the release and licence provisions for offences committed before 4 April 2005 where such provisions differ from those in Chapter 6 of Part 12 of the 2003 Act. Further amendments to the 2003 Act will:

- make the crediting of remand time an administrative function (rather than dependent on a direction of the court);

- simplify the calculation of crediting periods of remand on bail;

- provide for the unconditional release of prisoners serving sentences of less than 12 months at the half-way point of sentence;

- provide for additional restrictions for early release on Home Detention Curfew ("HDC");

- make provision for a revocation of a licence to be cancelled where a mistake was made;

- remove some of the restrictions on the use of recalls subject to automatic release;

- allow for the executive release of recalled extended sentence prisoners (subject to a risk test);

- make it clear that, where a prisoner is released on HDC before their automatic release date, a recall under section 254 during the HDC period will override automatic release when that date arrives, so that prisoners who have been recalled for misbehaviour may be detained beyond that date;

- prevent prisoners recalled during their HDC period being re-released prior to their automatic release date unless satisfactory arrangements for further HDC electronic monitoring can be put in place;

- provide for supervision of young adult prisoners on release from sentences of less than 12 months; and

- allow for foreign national prisoners serving indeterminate sentences to be removed from the United Kingdom when the tariff set by the court expires.

Chapter 5: Dangerous offenders

44. Chapter 5 repeals provisions in the 2003 Act creating indeterminate sentences for public protection and extended sentences and replaces them with provisions for life sentences to be imposed on conviction for a second serious offence and new provision for extended sentences. Equivalent provision is made for service law. The Chapter also creates a new power for the Secretary of State to amend the Parole Board release test for prisoners serving Indeterminate Sentences for Public Protection ("IPP"), extended sentence prisoners and determinate sentence prisoners subject to transitional provisions.

Chapter 6: Prisoners etc

45. Chapter 6 gives the Secretary of State the power to make rules in respect of the employment and payment of prisoners and persons in young offender institutions aged 18 or over, including in respect of reductions in, deductions from or levies upon such payments.

46. Chapter 6 also includes amendments to the Repatriation of Prisoners Act 1984, which governs the transfer of prisoners to and from the United Kingdom. The amendments provide for transit through Great Britain of prisoners serving sentences of imprisonment and statutory protection from prosecution of prisoners transferred to Great Britain under international prisoner transfer arrangements.

Chapter 7: Out of court disposals

47. Chapter 7 contains amendments to the legislation under which police constables may issue a penalty notice for disorder ("PND") and authorised persons may give conditional cautions. This includes the introduction of a PND with an education option and provision for conditional cautions to be given without the need to refer the case to the relevant prosecutor. The amendments also allow new types of conditions to be attached to a conditional caution given to a foreign offender without leave to enter or remain in the United Kingdom. The Chapter creates a new kind of youth

caution. It also makes amendments to youth conditional cautions, intended to make them more flexible.

Chapter 8: Rehabilitation of offenders

48.   Chapter 8 contains a package of changes to the Rehabilitation of Offenders Act 1974 ("the ROA") to amend the scope of the Act and its rehabilitation periods. The amendments extend the scope of the ROA so that custodial sentences of up to and including 4 years in length can become 'spent'. The times at which different convictions become 'spent' are also amended, and in most cases the rehabilitation periods are reduced. Where a caution or conviction has become spent, the offender is treated as rehabilitated in respect of that offence and is not obliged to declare it for most purposes, for example, when applying for employment or insurance.

Chapter 9: Offences

49.   Chapter 9 creates new offences of threatening with an offensive weapon or an article with a blade or point thereby creating an immediate risk of serious physical harm with a maximum penalty of 4 years imprisonment. There will be a minimum sentence of 6 months imprisonment for persons aged 18 or over found guilty of this new offence (unless this would be unjust in all the circumstances) and a minimum sentence for persons aged 16 and 17 years old of a 4 month detention and training order (again, unless it would be unjust in the circumstances).

50.   It creates a new offence of causing serious injury by dangerous driving and a criminal offence of squatting in a residential building.

51.   It amends the Scrap Metal Dealers Act 1964, including by creating a new offence of buying scrap metal for cash. The new offence prohibits scrap metal dealers paying for scrap metal other than by cheque or by electronic transfer.

52.   It contains provision amending section 76 of the Criminal Justice and Immigration Act 2008 ("the 2008 Act") (reasonable force for the purposes of self-defence etc).

TERRITORIAL EXTENT AND APPLICATION

53.   Section 152 sets out the territorial extent of the Act.

54.   The majority of the Act's provisions extend to England and Wales only, but certain provisions also extend to Scotland or Northern Ireland or both. The Act addresses non-devolved and devolved matters.

Provisions in the Act that extend to Northern Ireland

55.   The following provisions extending to Northern Ireland relate to excepted matters:

- Schedule 8 amends the Court Martial Appeals Act 1968 and aligns the availability of legal costs under that Act with the availability of legal costs in criminal proceedings in England and Wales under the Prosecution of Offences Act 1985, as amended by the Act.

- Section 140 relates to immigration and nationality proceedings. It amends the UK Borders Act 2007 to exclude immigration or nationality decision making, including initial decisions and any subsequent proceedings, from the operation of the Rehabilitation of Offenders Act 1974.

56. The following provisions extending to Northern Ireland relate to transferred matters:

- Section 22 enables the Director of Legal Aid Casework and others to obtain access to benefits information from the Department for Social Development in Northern Ireland and the Department of Finance and Personnel in Northern Ireland for the purpose of assessing individual financial eligibility for criminal and civil legal aid.

- Section 33 restricts the circumstances in which information provided under section 22 can be disclosed, including providing a criminal offence for disclosure in contravention of section 33.

- Section 40 and Schedule 6 make provision about sharing benefits information in relation to checking a person's financial eligibility for legal aid in Northern Ireland in two ways. First, they allow the chief executive of the Northern Ireland Legal Aid Commission (or other prescribed person) to request information from the Secretary of State and the Commissioners for Her Majesty's Revenue and Customs. Second, they allow the chief executive of the Northern Ireland Legal Aid Commission (or other prescribed person) to request information from the Department for Social Development in Northern Ireland and the Department of Finance and Personnel in Northern Ireland.

57. As these provisions relate to devolved matters, they required the consent of the Northern Ireland Assembly through a legislative consent motion. This was agreed to on 17 October 2011.

Provisions in the Act that extend to Scotland

58. The following provisions extend to Scotland and relate to reserved matters:

- Schedule 8 amends the Court Martial Appeals Act 1968 and aligns the availability of legal costs under that Act with the availability of legal costs in criminal proceedings in England and Wales under the Prosecution of Offences Act 1985, as amended by the Act.

- Section 140 relates to immigration and nationality proceedings. It amends the UK Borders Act 2007 to exclude immigration or nationality decision making, including initial decisions and any subsequent proceedings, from the operation of "the ROA 1974".

- Section 143 creates a new offence of causing serious injury by dangerous driving. The offence will extend to Scotland as well as England and Wales. The offence amends the Road Traffic Act 1988 ("RTA") and requires consequential amendments to the Road Traffic Offenders Act 1988 ("RTOA"). The subject matter of this legislation is reserved.

59.	Sections 130 and 131 relate to the transfer of prisoners into and out of Great Britain. International relations, including the negotiation of prisoner transfer arrangements are a reserved matter. However, consideration of individual transfers is a devolved matter. Sections 130 and 131 make amendments to the Repatriation of Prisoners Act 1984. At the request of the Scottish Executive these amendments will apply to Scotland. The Sewel Convention provides that Westminster will not normally legislate with regard to devolved matters in Scotland without the consent of the Scottish Parliament. A Legislative Consent Motion in this respect was passed by the Scottish Parliament on 7 December 2012.

Provisions in the Act that apply in Wales

60.	The provisions in the Act relate to non-devolved matters in Wales. The Act does not affect the powers of Welsh Ministers and does not make different provision in relation to England and Wales.

COMMENTARY

Part 1: Legal Aid
Provision of legal aid
Section 1: Lord Chancellor's functions

61.	Section 1 gives the Lord Chancellor overall responsibility for legal aid.

62.	*Subsection (1)* provides that the Lord Chancellor must secure that legal aid is made available in accordance with Part 1 of the Act. "Legal aid" is defined in *subsection (2)* as civil legal services and advice, assistance and representation for criminal investigations and proceedings that are required to be made available under sections 9, 10, 13, 15 or 16 or paragraphs 3 to 5 of Schedule 3.

63.	*Subsections (3) and (4)* ensure that the Lord Chancellor has the power to arrange for the provision of general information about the law and legal system, including information about where people may obtain advice and assistance about the law and legal system, and to perform functions that support the Lord Chancellor's functions in relation to legal aid. For example, the Lord Chancellor may make arrangements for a legal advice helpline which, as well as assisting people who qualify for legal aid, would also be able to assist callers who do not qualify for legal aid by referring them to providers of appropriate services.

Section 2: Arrangements

64.	Section 2 makes provision about the arrangements the Lord Chancellor may enter into in order to fulfil the Lord Chancellor's duty in section 1 to secure the availability of legal aid and for the purposes of carrying out the Lord Chancellor's other functions under this Part.

65.	As a Minister of the Crown, the Lord Chancellor has power, for example, to enter into contracts relating to the Lord Chancellor's functions. *Subsection (1)* ensures the Lord Chancellor may make any other arrangements appropriate for fulfilling the Lord Chancellor's functions in relation to legal aid and *subsection (2)* ensures that arrangements the Lord Chancellor may enter into include arrangements of the type referred to in *subsection (2)*, such as establishing a body to provide services.

66.   *Subsection (3)* allows the Lord Chancellor to make regulations about remuneration for those providing legal aid services. Section 42(1) provides that remuneration includes disbursements. This would include, for example, power to set the level of fees for lawyers and experts who are providing such services. Where such fee levels are set in regulations, or in other arrangements (such as contracts) made by the Lord Chancellor in relation to legal aid, *subsection (4)* provides that if the Lord Chancellor makes arrangements for a court, tribunal or other person to assess such remuneration, the court, tribunal or other person must apply the remuneration levels set by the Lord Chancellor.

67.   *Subsection (5)* allows the Lord Chancellor to make different arrangements for the provision of legal aid in relation to different areas in England and Wales, different types of case and different classes of person. This provides flexibility including, where appropriate, to pilot arrangements.

Section 3: Standards of service

68.   Section 3 makes provision about setting and monitoring standards of legal aid services.

69.   *Subsections (1) and (2)* enable the Lord Chancellor to set quality standards for those providing or wishing to provide legal aid services and to establish a system of accreditation of those providers. Accreditation may be by the Lord Chancellor or by persons authorised by the Lord Chancellor. Any accreditation arrangements must make provision about the monitoring of the services provided by those who are accredited and for the withdrawal of accreditation if the services are unsatisfactory.

70.   *Subsections (4) and (5)* allow the Lord Chancellor, and those authorised by the Lord Chancellor, to make charges in connection with accreditation and monitoring.

Section 4: Director of Legal Aid Casework

71.   Section 4 makes provision about the Director of Legal Aid Casework, a statutory office holder.

72.   *Subsection (1)* requires the Lord Chancellor to designate a civil servant as the Director of Legal Aid Casework. The Director's function is to make decisions on legal aid in individual cases.

73.   To enable the Director to perform their functions, *subsection (2)* requires the Lord Chancellor to provide civil servants or other persons to give appropriate assistance to the Director.

74.   *Subsection (3)* requires the Director to comply with directions given by the Lord Chancellor and to have regard to guidance issued by the Lord Chancellor. *Subsection (5)* requires the Lord Chancellor to publish such guidance and directions. Examples of directions which may be given include directions about the delegation of the

Director's functions under section 5 and directions about determinations in respect of exceptional cases under section 10.

75. *Subsection (4)(a)* provides that the Lord Chancellor may not give a direction or guidance under *subsection (3)* in relation to an individual case. *Subsection (4)(b)* places a duty on the Lord Chancellor to ensure that the Director acts independently of the Lord Chancellor when applying directions or guidance under *subsection (3)* in relation to an individual case.

76. *Subsection (5)* provides that the Lord Chancellor must publish any directions and guidance given under this section.

Section 5: Delegation

77. Section 5 makes provision about the delegation of the Lord Chancellor's and Director's functions.

78. *Subsection (1)* allows the Lord Chancellor to delegate the functions of the Lord Chancellor under section 1(3), which would include aspects of the civil legal advice telephone helpline, and under section 3, which may include delegating the accreditation and monitoring function to an outside organisation.

79. *Subsection (2)* allows the Lord Chancellor to make regulations providing for any functions that may be given to the Lord Chancellor under regulations made under Part 1 of the Act to be exercisable by a person authorised by the Lord Chancellor or employees of such a person.

80. *Subsection (3)* allows the Director to delegate the Director's functions. This enables the Director to delegate, for example, decision-making in relation to the merits of a legal aid application, the application of any relevant means test for a particular area of work in relation to a legal aid application and the on-going monitoring of decisions.

81. *Subsection (4)* enables the Lord Chancellor to make regulations providing for functions conferred on the Director under regulations made under Part 1 of the Act to be exercisable by a person authorised by the Director or an employee of such a person.

82. *Subsection (5)* provides that under section 4 the Lord Chancellor may give directions to the Director about the delegation of the Director's functions. The Lord Chancellor will be able to require the Director to delegate, or not to delegate, particular functions and to give directions about the persons to whom the Director may or may not delegate those functions.

83. *Subsections (6) to (8)* ensure that a function of the Lord Chancellor or Director may be delegated entirely or subject to limitations or conditions. For example, decision-making in relation to the merits and financial eligibility might be delegated to providers in relation to particular matters, or subject to particular financial limits as to the amount of work that can be carried out before the case must be referred to the Director for a decision on further legal aid funding.

Section 6: Authorisations

84.   Section 6 makes provision about the effect of the delegation of functions under section 5.

85.   *Subsection (1)* gives the Lord Chancellor and the Director the power to limit the duration of a delegation as well as to vary or revoke the delegation at any time. It also reserves the right of the Lord Chancellor and the Director (or another person) to continue to exercise a function that has been delegated.

86.   *Subsections (2) and (3)* provide that any act or omission by a person ("authorised person") in exercising a function of the Lord Chancellor or Director delegated to them under section 5 is to be treated as being done or omitted to be done by the Lord Chancellor or the Director.

87.   However the liability of the Lord Chancellor or Director for acts or omissions of an authorised person is not absolute. *Subsection (4)* provides that *subsections (2) and (3)* do not affect the rights and liabilities of the Lord Chancellor and the authorised person between themselves (for example, contractual disputes), do not prevent civil proceedings from being brought against the authorised person, do not apply to criminal offences alleged to have been committed by the authorised person and do not make the Lord Chancellor or Director liable under section 6 of the Human Rights Act 1998 for acts of the authorised person which are private in nature.

Section 7: Annual report

88.   Section 7 concerns the production of an annual report by the Director of Legal Aid Casework.

89.   *Subsection (1)* requires the Director to produce an annual report for each financial year as soon as practicable following the end of that financial year.

90.   *Subsection (2)* requires that the report set out how the Director has carried out the functions of the office in the financial year. *Subsections (3)* and *(4)* respectively require that the Director send a copy of the report to the Lord Chancellor, and that the Lord Chancellor lay the report before Parliament and arrange for its publication.

Civil legal aid
Section 8: Civil legal services

91.   Section 8 defines civil legal services for the purposes of Part 1.

92.   *Subsections (1)* and *(2)* explain what is meant by "legal services", namely services comprising advice and assistance provided in relation to the law as it applies to a particular case, legal proceedings and the resolution of legal disputes. Those services include, in particular, representation and mediation (and other forms of dispute resolution).

93.   *Subsection (3)* provides that "civil legal services" are all legal services other than those services that are required to be made available under the provisions about criminal legal aid. This is in order to avoid any overlap between civil and criminal legal aid.

Section 9: General cases

94.   Section 9 makes provision about when civil legal services are to be made available.

95.   *Subsection (1)* provides that civil legal services are to be made available subject to two conditions. The first is they are civil legal services described in Part 1 of Schedule 1 to the Act. The second is that the Director has determined, in accordance with the provisions of this Part of the Act, that the individual qualifies for those legal services and the Director has not withdrawn that determination (that is, the individual continues to qualify for those services).

96.   *Subsection (2)* provides the Lord Chancellor with the power to add services to Part 1 of Schedule 1 or to vary or remove services described there. He would be able to do so by modifying Part 1, 2, 3 or 4 of Schedule 1. This will be subject to the affirmative procedure.

97.   Section 9 and Part 1 of Schedule 1 reverse the arrangements in the Access to Justice Act 1999, which provided for civil legal aid to be available in relation any matter not excluded by Schedule 2 to that Act. Under this Act, the types of case for which legal aid may be made available are set out in Part 1 of Schedule 1.

Schedule 1: Civil legal services
Introduction

98.   Each paragraph of Part 1 of Schedule 1 describes a type of civil legal services that may be made available under the Act. Each paragraph is subject to exclusions – either exclusions specific to the paragraph or the general exclusions set out in Parts 2 and 3 of the Schedule. For example, paragraph 2 of Part 1 of Schedule 1 describes civil legal services provided in relation to matters relating to special educational needs. It states that the exclusions in Part 2 and 3 of the Schedule apply.

99.   Part 2 of Schedule 1 lists civil legal services that are not to be available, even where they might otherwise fall within the descriptions of services in Part 1. Some paragraphs in Part 1 provide exceptions from the exclusions in Part 2, so that one or more of the general exclusions are disapplied. For example, under paragraph 41 of Part 1 of Schedule 1 civil legal services provided to an individual in relation to an inquest under the Coroners Act 1988 into the death of a member of the individual's immediate family can be made available. However, the services provided cannot include the services listed in Part 2, with the exception of civil legal services provided in relation to personal injury or death. This means that civil legal services in relation to death could be made available by virtue of paragraph 41 of Part 1.

100.   Part 3 of Schedule 1 provides that the civil legal services listed in Part 1 of Schedule 1 do not include advocacy unless: (1) the type of advocacy in question is listed in Part 3 of the Schedule, except to the extent that Part 1 of Schedule 1 provides otherwise; or (2) Part 1 of Schedule 1 makes specific provision bringing other types of advocacy within scope for that particular matter which are not listed in Part 3 of the Schedule. Section 42(1) defines advocacy as meaning the exercise of a right of audience before a court, tribunal or other person.

101.   Part 4 of Schedule 1 makes provision about the interpretation of Schedule 1. Paragraph 1 of Part 4 provides that if one paragraph of Part 1 includes a type of civil legal service which is either expressly or impliedly excluded by another paragraph of Part 1, that type of service is still a type of civil legal service that may be made available The remainder of Part 4 of Schedule 1 makes further provision about the interpretation of references to legislation and services that appear in the Schedule.

102.   Schedule 1 includes a number of powers for the Lord Chancellor to make regulations to clarify or adjust particular paragraphs. For example, under paragraph 6 of Part 1 civil legal services provided in relation to community care services can be made available. Paragraph 6(3) defines community care services as services which a relevant person may provide under a number of listed enactments. The definition of "relevant person" allows other relevant persons to be prescribed.

103.   There is a table setting out the contents of Schedule 1 at Annex B and a more detailed explanation of the paragraphs in Schedule 1 at Annex C.

Section 10: Exceptional cases

104.   Section 10 gives the Director the power to provide individuals with civil legal services not included in Schedule 1 in exceptional circumstances subject to certain conditions.

105.   *Subsections (1) and (2)* provide that civil legal services not included in Schedule 1 are to be provided to an individual if the Director has, first, made an exceptional case determination and, second, determined that the individual qualifies for those services (provided that neither determination has been withdrawn).

106.   *Subsection (3)(a)* provides that an exceptional case determination is a determination by the Director that it is necessary to make legal services available to an individual because the failure to do so would amount to a breach of the individual's Convention rights (as defined in s.1(1) of the Human Rights Act 1998) or any rights of the individual to the provision of legal services that are enforceable EU rights (as defined in section 2(1) of the European Communities Act 1972).

107.   It will be necessary to make legal services available to an individual where the withholding of such services would clearly amount to a breach of Article 6 of the ECHR ('right to a fair trial'), Article 2 of the ECHR ('right to life') or any other provision of the Convention giving rise to an obligation to provide such services. There will be a breach of the enforceable EU rights of the individual to the provision of legal services where the withholding of such services would be clearly contrary to the rights reaffirmed by Article 47 of the Charter of Fundamental Rights, or to the rights to legal services that are conferred on individuals by EU instruments.

108.   *Subsection (3)(b)* provides that an exceptional case determination may also be made where the Director considers that the failure to provide legal services would not necessarily amount to a breach of an individual's rights, but that it is nevertheless appropriate for the services to be made available, having regard to the risk of such a breach occurring.

109.   *Subsections (1) and (4)* provide that advocacy services are to be made available to an individual for the purposes of an inquest under the Coroners Act 1988 into the death of a member of that individual's family if the Director, first, has made a wider public interest determination in relation to the individual and the inquest and, second, has determined that the individual qualifies for the services (provided that neither determination has been withdrawn). *Subsection (4)* does not preclude the making available of advocacy services in such inquest proceedings by virtue of an exceptional case determination under *subsection (3)*.

110.   *Subsection (5)* provides that a wider public interest determination may be made in relation to advocacy for the purposes of an inquest into the death of a member of an individual's family where, in the particular circumstances of the case, the provision of advocacy is likely to produce significant benefits for a class of person other than the individual or the individual's family.

111.   *Subsection (6)* defines when one individual is a member of another individual's family for the purposes of this section.

Section 11: Qualifying for civil legal aid

112.   Section 11 makes provision about how the Director must determine whether an individual qualifies for civil legal services.

113.   *Subsection (1)* provides that in determining whether an individual qualifies for civil legal services, the Director must apply the provisions about means testing (section 21) and the merits criteria set out in regulations prepared by the Lord Chancellor.

114.   *Subsection (2)* provides that when setting the criteria, the Lord Chancellor must consider the circumstances in which it is appropriate to make civil legal services available. It also provides that, in setting the criteria, the Lord Chancellor must in particular consider the extent to which they ought to reflect the factors set out in *subsection (3)*. The factors in *subsection (3)* are similar to the factors that the LSC is currently required to consider when setting the Funding Code criteria under section 8(2) of the Access to Justice Act 1999.

115.   *Subsection (4)* provides that if more than one type of service is available for an individual, then the Lord Chancellor, in setting the criteria, must aim to ensure that the individual qualifies for the most appropriate service in all the circumstances (having regard to the criteria).

116.   *Subsection (5)* requires the regulations to reflect the principle that, in many disputes, mediation and other forms of dispute resolution are more appropriate than court proceedings.

Section 12: Determinations

117.   Section 12 makes provision about the procedure for determinations made by the Director about whether an individual qualifies for civil legal aid.

118. *Subsection (1)* provides that in such a determination the Director must state the type of services (for example, advice and assistance) and for what those services are to be available (for example, a claim for judicial review). The Director will be also be able to set out in the determination any qualifications or exclusions that apply.

119. *Subsection (2)* provides that the Lord Chancellor may make regulations about determinations and the withdrawal of determinations. *Subsections (3) to (5)* make further provision about those regulations.

120. *Subsection (3)* provides that the regulations may include provision about the form and content of applications and determinations (for example specifying an application form) and provision that an application or determination may or must be made and withdrawn in writing, by telephone or by other prescribed means. The regulations may also include provision about time limits, provision about conditions that must be satisfied by an applicant before a determination is made, provision requiring information and documents to be provided, provision about when a determination may or must be withdrawn, provision requiring applicants to be given reasons for the making or withdrawal of a determination and provision about giving information to unsuccessful applicants about other ways in which they might obtain the advice they are seeking. This is similar to the provision about procedure that may be made in the LSC's Funding Code (see section 8(5) of the Access to Justice Act 1999).

121. *Subsection (4)* ensures that circumstances in which a determination may or must be withdrawn can relate to compliance by the individual with requirements imposed on the individual under Part 1 of the Act, for example, to provide information or to make a payment under section 23.

122. *Subsection (5)* requires the regulations to include provision about the review of determinations and of the withdrawal of determinations. *Subsection (6)* enables the regulations to include provision about appeals against determinations and against the withdrawal of determinations.

Criminal legal aid
Section 13: Advice and assistance for individuals in custody
123. Section 13 makes provision about initial advice and assistance for an individual who is arrested and held in custody at a police station or other premises.

124. The current provision governing police station advice and assistance is at section 13(1)(a) of the Access to Justice Act 1999.

125. *Subsection (1)* requires initial advice and assistance to be made available to individuals who are arrested and held in custody at a police station or other premises if the Director has determined that the individual qualifies for advice and assistance and has not withdrawn that determination. "Initial advice" and "initial assistance" are defined in *subsection (7)* as the sort of advice and assistance that an individual might need while in custody. *Subsection (8)* enables the Lord Chancellor to make regulations providing that certain advice and assistance is not initial advice and assistance for the purposes of this section.

126. In making a determination, *subsection (2)* places a duty on the Director to have regard to the interests of justice.

127. *Subsection (3)* provides that any determination under this section must specify the types of advice or assistance to be made available. *Subsection (4)* provides that the Lord Chancellor may make regulations about determinations and the withdrawal of determinations. *Subsections (5) and (6)* make further provision about the procedure for determinations under this section.

128. *Subsection (5)* provides that the regulations may include provision about the form and content of applications and determinations (for example specifying an application form) and about how an application or determination must be made or withdrawn. The regulations may also include provision about time limits, provision about conditions that must be satisfied by an applicant before a determination is made, provision requiring information and documents to be provided, provision about when a determination may or must be withdrawn and provision requiring applicants to be given reasons for the making or withdrawal of a determination.

129. *Subsection (6)* ensures that circumstances in which a determination may or must be withdrawn can relate to compliance by the individual with requirements imposed on the individual under Part 1 of the Act, for example, to provide information under section 23.

Section 14: Criminal proceedings

130. Section 14 defines "criminal proceedings" for the purposes of this Part of the Act and is based on the existing provision at section 12(2) of the Access to Justice Act 1999.

131. "Criminal proceedings" include criminal trials (section 14(a)), sentencing hearings (section 14(b)), extradition hearings (section 14(c)), binding over proceedings (section 14(d)), appeals on behalf of a convicted person who has died (section 14(e)), proceedings on a reference on a point of law following acquittal on indictment (section 14(f)) and proceedings for contempt in the face of a court (section 14(g)). Section 14(h) allows the Lord Chancellor to specify in secondary legislation further types of proceedings that are to be considered to be criminal proceedings for the purposes of this Part of the Act.

Section 15: Advice and assistance for criminal proceedings

132. Section 15 gives the Lord Chancellor the power to prescribe in regulations when advice and assistance must be made available to individuals in connection with criminal proceedings (*subsection (1)*). The power broadly reflects the provision about advice and assistance in section 13(1)(b) of the Access to Justice Act 1999.

133. *Subsection (2)* describes the individuals in respect of whom provision can be made under this section. It covers those involved in investigations that could lead to criminal proceedings (other than where the individual has been arrested and held in custody), those who are before a court, tribunal or other person in criminal proceedings, and those who have been the subject of criminal proceedings.

134. When making the regulations, the Lord Chancellor must take into account the interests of justice (*subsection (3)*) and the regulations must require the Director, in making a determination whether an individual qualifies for advice and assistance, to take into account the interests of justice (*subsection (4)*).

135. *Subsection (5)* provides that the regulations may also require the Director, in making determinations, to apply the means testing provisions (section 21) and any other criteria specified in the regulations.

136. *Subsection (6)* provides that the regulations may make provision about determinations and the withdrawal of determinations. *Subsections (7) to (9)* make further provision about the procedure for determinations under this section.

137. *Subsection (7)* provides that the regulations may include provision about the form and content of applications and determinations (for example specifying an application form) and provision that an application or determination may or must be made and withdrawn in writing, by telephone or by other prescribed means. The regulations may also include provision about time limits, provision about conditions that must be satisfied by an applicant before a determination is made, provision requiring information and documents to be provided, provision about when a determination may or must be withdrawn, and provision requiring applicants to be given reasons for the making or withdrawal of a determination.

138. *Subsection (8)* ensures that circumstances in which a determination may or must be withdrawn can relate to compliance by the individual with requirements imposed on the individual under Part 1 of the Act, for example, to provide information or to make a payment under section 23.

139. *Subsection (9)* provides that the regulations may make provision about reviews of and appeals to a court, tribunal or other person against a decision of the Director that an individual does not qualify for advice and assistance on the grounds that the interests of justice or other criteria set out in regulations made under *subsection (5)(b)* are not met.

140. *Subsection (10)* ensures that under this section "assistance" can include advocacy (as defined in section 42(1)) undertaken on behalf of the individual.

Section 16: Representation for criminal proceedings
141. Section 16 identifies the circumstances and conditions under which representation for the purposes of criminal proceedings is to be made available.

142. *Subsection (1)* provides that representation is to be available if the individual is a specified individual in relation to the proceedings (see *subsection (6)*) and the Director or, as the case may be, a court has determined, provisionally or otherwise, that the individual qualifies for representation.

143. *Subsection (2)* requires representation for the purposes of criminal proceedings to be made available on appeal to the Crown Court to private prosecutors whom the Director or court has determined, provisionally or otherwise, qualify for such representation.

144. *Subsection (3)* provides that where an individual qualifies for representation for the purposes of criminal proceedings, representation is also to be made available for the purposes of any related bail proceedings as well as any preliminary or incidental proceedings. *Subsection (4)* enables the Lord Chancellor in secondary legislation to specify whether proceedings are or are not preliminary or incidental for this purpose and also to make exceptions to *subsection (3)*. Under the current regulations made under the Access to Justice Act 1999, for example, proceedings dealing with an individual for non-compliance with a Crown Court order are not to be regarded as incidental.

145. *Subsection (5)* provides that regulations under *subsection (4)(b)* making exceptions from *subsection (3)* may make provision by reference to proceedings that take place more than a specific period of time before or after the main proceedings. This would allow, for example, a period of time to be specified after which the original determination on representation would not cover advice on an appeal or after which a new determination would be needed for the purposes of applying to vary or appeal against an order made at the conclusion of the proceedings.

Section 17: Qualifying for representation
146. Section 17 makes provision about how the Director or a court must make determinations about whether an individual qualifies for representation for the purposes of criminal proceedings.

147. *Subsection (1)* requires the Director or a court to determine (whether provisionally or otherwise) whether an individual qualifies for representation by applying the means testing provisions (section 21) and the interests of justice test provided for in *subsection (2)*.

148. *Subsection (2)* sets out the factors that are to be considered in assessing whether an individual meets the interests of justice. These mirror the existing provision at paragraph 5 of Schedule 3 to the Access to Justice Act 1999. *Subsection (3)* enables the Lord Chancellor to add to or vary these factors. The Lord Chancellor may also make regulations specifying circumstances in which the interests of justice will be considered to be met (*subsection (4)*).

Section 18: Determinations by Director
149. Section 18 makes provision about the power of the Director to make determinations about representation for the purposes of criminal proceedings and the procedure to be followed.

150. *Subsection (1)* provides that the Director may determine whether an individual is eligible for representation for criminal proceedings unless a court is authorised to do so under section 19. This reverses the default position in the Access to Justice Act

1999 where the decision as to whether to grant legal aid is for the court unless the LSC is given the power to make the decision. However, over recent years, most decision-making powers have transferred in practice to the LSC and there are now only limited circumstances in which the court can make a determination.

151. *Subsection (2)* requires the Director, in the determination, to specify the criminal proceedings in respect of which the individual qualifies for representation. *Subsection (3)* provides that the regulations may make provision about determinations and the withdrawal of determinations. *Subsections (4) to (7)* make further provision about the procedure for determinations under this section.

152. *Subsection (4)* provides that the regulations may include provision about the form and content of applications and determinations and provision that an application or determination must be made and withdrawn in writing, by telephone or by other prescribed means. The regulations may also include provision about time limits, provision about conditions that must be satisfied by an applicant before a determination is made, provision requiring information and documents to be provided, provision about when a determination may or must be withdrawn, and provision requiring applicants to be given reasons for the making or withdrawal of determinations. Provision may also be made about the review of a decision by the Director that the individual does not qualify, or no longer qualifies, for representation on the grounds that the interests of justice are not met.

153. *Subsection (5)* ensures that circumstances in which a determination may or must be withdrawn can relate to compliance by the individual with requirements imposed on the individual under Part 1 of the Act, for example, to provide information or to make a payment under section 23.

154. *Subsection (6)* provides that in cases where representation is refused or withdrawn on the grounds that the interests of justice do not require it, the individual has a right of appeal to a court, tribunal or other person prescribed by regulations. The right of appeal is subject to exceptions specified in regulations under *subsection (7)*.

155. *Subsection (8)* provides that this section does not authorise the Director to make a provisional determination, and as such any reference to a determination in this section does not include a provisional determination. Section 20 makes provision about provisional determinations.

Section 19: Determinations by court

156. Section 19 makes provision about the power of a court to make determinations about representation for the purposes of criminal proceedings and the procedure to be followed.

157. *Subsection (1)* enables the Lord Chancellor to make regulations providing for a court to determine whether an individual qualifies for representation. Under the current provisions made under the Access to Justice Act 1999, the Crown Court may grant a representation order for contempt proceedings, for proceedings that arise from an alleged failure to comply with an order of the Crown Court where it appears to the court that there is no time to instruct a solicitor and for proceedings where the

individual is brought before the court following the issue of a bench warrant. The High Court and the Court of Appeal (Criminal Division) may grant a representation order for proceedings before those courts and the Supreme Court.

158. *Subsection (2)* enables regulations to make provision about the procedure for determinations, including the form of the application to the court and the form of the determination of the court, provision that applications and determinations may or must be made and withdrawn in writing, by telephone or by other prescribed means, and provision about time limits and circumstances in which a determination may or must be withdrawn.

159. *Subsection (3)* ensures that the circumstances in which a determination may or must be withdrawn may relate to whether an individual has complied with requirements imposed on them under Part 1, for example, a requirement to provide documents or to make a payment under section 23.

160. *Subsection (4)* requires the regulations to provide that, subject to prescribed exceptions, in cases where representation is refused on the grounds that the interests of justice do not require it, the individual has a right of appeal to such court, tribunal or other person, as may be prescribed.

161. *Subsection (6)* provides that regulations under this section may not authorise a court to make a provisional determination, and as such any reference to a determination in this section does not include a provisional determination. Section 20 makes provision about provisional determinations.

Section 20: Provisional determinations
162. Section 20 makes provision about the power of the Director or a court to make a provisional determination about whether an individual qualifies for representation in certain cases. This reflects paragraph 1A of Schedule 3 to the Access to Justice Act 1999.

163. *Subsection (1)* enables the Lord Chancellor to make regulations to allow the Director or a court to make a provisional determination about whether an individual qualifies for representation where the individual is involved in an investigation which may result in criminal proceedings, the determination is for the purposes of criminal proceedings that may result from that investigation and other specified conditions are met. A provisional grant of a representation order is currently permitted in investigations where the prosecution has initiated plea discussions under the Attorney General's Guidelines on Plea Discussions in Cases of Serious or Complex Fraud.

164. *Subsection (2)* provides that the regulations may make provision about the stage of an investigation when a provisional determination may be made, provision about when the provisional determination becomes a full determination and ceases to be provisional, and provision about the withdrawal of a provisional determination.

Financial resources
Section 21: Financial resources

165. Section 21 relates to financial eligibility for legal aid services. In the Access to Justice Act 1999 separate provision is made in respect of financial eligibility for different types of legal aid (in section 7, in respect of civil legal aid and in paragraph 3B of Schedule 3, in respect of criminal legal aid in the form of representation). This section contains provisions on financial eligibility that are applicable to both civil and criminal legal aid.

166. *Subsection (1)* specifies the basic rule, applicable to both civil and criminal aid, that legal aid will only be granted to an individual who is determined to be financially eligible for the services. As under the Access to Justice Act 1999, the financial eligibility rules will be contained in regulations made by the Lord Chancellor (see *subsection (2)*). The basic rule in *subsection (1)* applies to decisions on granting civil legal aid and decisions on granting criminal legal aid for representation in criminal proceedings. It also applies to decisions on granting criminal legal aid for advice and assistance for criminal proceedings, if regulations under section 15 provide for that *(see the definition of a "relevant determination" in *subsection (8))*.

167. *Subsection (2)(b)* makes clear that regulations may provide for exceptions from the basic rule, so that an individual may receive certain services regardless of their financial means.

168. *Subsections (3) and (4)* enable regulations to provide that an individual is to be treated as having or not having particular financial resources, including providing that an individual is to be treated as having financial resources of a person of a specified description. This allows, for example, for regulations on financial eligibility to provide that the resources of the partner of a legal aid applicant are to be treated as the resources of the applicant.

169. *Subsections (5) and (6)* enable regulations to make provision about making and withdrawing financial eligibility determinations. *Subsection (6)* is a non-exhaustive list of matters that such regulations may contain, including provision requiring information and documents to be provided and provision establishing procedures for the review of financial eligibility determinations.

Section 22: Information about financial resources

170. Section 22 provides a gateway for the disclosure of information to the Director (or other prescribed person) by the Secretary of State (in practice, the Secretary of State for Work and Pensions), the Commissioners for Her Majesty's Revenue and Customs ("the Commissioners"), the Department for Social Development in Northern Ireland or the Department of Finance and Personnel in Northern Ireland (a "relevant Northern Ireland Department").

171. *Subsection (1)* enables the Director (or other prescribed person) to make a request for certain information to the Secretary of State, a relevant Northern Ireland Department or the Commissioners. *Subsection (2)* provides that such a request may only be made for the purpose of facilitating a determination about an individual's means, that is, for the purpose of finding out whether they are financially eligible for legal aid.

172.   *Subsection (3)* lists the categories of information which may be requested from the Secretary of State or the relevant Northern Ireland Department. It includes a power to add further categories of information by secondary legislation.

173.   *Subsection (4)* sets out the categories of information which may be requested from the Commissioners. It includes a power to add further categories of information by secondary legislation, with the Commissioners' consent (see *subsection (6)*).

174.   *Subsection (7)* provides that the Secretary of State, the relevant Northern Ireland Department and the Commissioners may disclose to the Director (or other prescribed person) information specified in an information request made under this section.

Contributions and costs
Section 23: Payment for services

175.   Section 23 concerns payments for services by legally aided individuals. The section largely reflects powers in sections 10, 17 and 17A of the Access to Justice Act 1999 and brings together provisions on payments for services into a single provision applicable (for the most part) to both civil and criminal legal aid.

176.   *Subsection (1)* sets out the basic rule that an individual who receives legal aid can only be required to make a payment in connection with the provision of the services where regulations require them to do so. Any regulations made under *subsection (1)* must provide for repayment to the individual of any amount paid by the individual that exceeds the amount required to be paid by regulations under this section and section 24 (see *subsection (11)*).

177.   *Subsection (2)* is a non-exhaustive list of ways in which regulations made under this section can require payments from individuals. Regulations can, in prescribed circumstances, require payment of the cost of the services, a contribution in respect of those costs or an amount in respect of administration costs.

178.   *Subsection (3)* permits regulations to provide that, in civil disputes only, legally aided individuals may be required to make a payment of an amount which exceeds the costs of the services provided. This allows for a so-called 'Supplementary Legal Aid Scheme' whereby a percentage of certain damages obtained by a successful legally-aided claimant may be required to be paid to a prescribed person, such as the Lord Chancellor. The response to the consultation paper *Proposals for the Reform of Legal Aid in England and Wales* confirmed the Government's intention to create such a scheme. There is an equivalent provision at section 10(2)(c) of the Access to Justice 1999.

179.   *Subsection (4)* permits regulations made under this section to include provision about how the costs of services made available to a legally-aided individual are to be determined. This reproduces provisions currently found in sections 10(6)(b), 17(3)(c) and 17A(2)(b) of the Access to Justice Act 1999.

180.   *Subsections (5), (8) and (9)* make further provisions about the contents of regulations that may be made under this section. Regulations may, for example, provide for liability to pay to arise on a determination by a prescribed person (as is currently the

case for criminal contributions and orders to pay costs) and for the variation or withdrawal of a determination about liability to make a payment. Regulations may also make provision for payment by periodical payments or lump sums out of income or capital and for procedural matters, such as when payment is to be made and to whom.

181.   *Subsections (6) and (7)* make provision in identical terms to section 21(3) and (4), explained at paragraph 168 above.

182.   *Subsection (10)* permits regulations to provide that a legally-aided individual can be required to pay interest on loans, payments required to be made after the provision of the relevant services and overdue payments. Similar provision is currently made in section 10(4) and section 17(2)(d) of the Access to Justice Act 1999.

Section 24: Enforcement
183.   Section 24 permits regulations to provide for the enforcement of a requirement to make a payment imposed by regulations under section 23. The regulations can include provision for the recovery of the costs of enforcement from the individual *(subsection (2))* and can require documents and information to be provided *(subsection (4))*.

184.   Under *subsection (3)* regulations will be able to provide that overdue sums are recoverable summarily as a civil debt, that is to say through magistrates' courts in accordance with the Magistrates' Courts Act 1980. The regulations will also be able to provide that overdue sums are recoverable, if the county court or High Court so orders, as if they were payable under an order of the High Court or county court in accordance with rule 70.5 of the Civil Procedure Rules, thereby making it unnecessary to begin fresh proceedings in respect of the debt. These provisions are similar to the regulation-making powers relating to criminal legal aid in sections 17(4) and 17A(2A) of the Access to Justice Act 1999 (as inserted by the Coroners and Justice Act 2009).

185.   *Subsection (5)* introduces Schedule 2.

Schedule 2: Criminal legal aid: motor vehicle orders
186.   Schedule 2 enables regulations to be made to authorise a court to make motor vehicle orders as a form of enforcement action in relation to criminal legal aid. "Motor vehicle orders" consist of clamping orders and vehicle sale orders. A clamping order is an order that a motor vehicle be fitted with an immobilisation device. Under a vehicle sale order, a motor vehicle which has been fitted with an immobilization device in accordance with enforcement regulations may be sold and the proceeds of sale may be applied in paying the overdue sum. Schedule 2 includes further detailed provision regarding the content of regulations about motor vehicle orders, including procedural matters and requirements that must be met before a court may make an order. Schedule 2 is based on provisions in section 17(2A) to (2E) of, and Schedule 3A to, the Access to Justice Act 1999 (as inserted by the Coroners and Justice Act 2009).

Section 25: Charges on property in connection with civil legal services

187. *Subsection (1)* provides for a statutory charge to arise on any property recovered or preserved by an individual in receipt of civil legal aid, including costs payable to the individual, whether the property or costs are recovered, preserved or payable following legal proceedings or as part of a compromise or settlement of a dispute. Such a charge currently arises under section 10(7) of the Access to Justice Act 1999.

188. *Subsection (2)* describes the amounts of money to which the statutory charge relates. These are the amounts spent by the Lord Chancellor in securing the provision of the civil legal services and any other amounts payable by the individual by virtue of sections 23 and 24. As under the Access to Justice Act 1999, regulations may make provision about the statutory charge. Such regulations can provide for circumstances in which the charge does not apply, provide for the charge to be in favour of the Lord Chancellor or the service provider, modify the charge for the purposes of its application in prescribed cases or circumstances, and provide for the enforcement of the charge (*subsections (3) and (4)*).

189. *Subsection (5)* permits regulations made for the purpose of enforcing the statutory charge to require amounts of money awarded or payable to the legally-aided individual to be paid to the Lord Chancellor or the service provider and to make provision about matters such as the timing and manner of payment, about how such monies are to be dealt with and about the enforcement of the requirement to pay.

Section 26: Costs in civil proceedings

190. Section 26 relates to costs in civil proceedings where a party is legally-aided and substantially reproduces provisions currently found in section 11 of the Access to Justice Act 1999.

191. *Subsection (1)* limits the costs that can be awarded against an individual receiving civil legal aid to the amount (if any) that is reasonable given the financial resources of both parties and their conduct during the case.

192. *Subsection (3)* provides that this protection may be disapplied by regulations.

193. Subject to the restriction in *subsection (1)*, regulations may be made under this section about costs in proceedings where an individual is in receipt of civil legal aid. Such regulations may, among other things, specify the principles that are to be applied in determining the amount of any costs awarded for or against a party receiving civil legal aid, limit the circumstances in which a costs order may be enforced against the individual receiving civil legal aid and make provision about when a court can require the Lord Chancellor to pay any costs incurred by the opponent of the legally-aided party (*subsections (5) and (6)*). *Subsections (7) and (8)* make provision in identical terms to section 21(3) and (4), explained at paragraph 168 above.

Providers of services etc

Section 27: Choice of provider of services etc

194. Section 27 makes provision about an individual's choice of provider of criminal and civil legal aid.

195.   *Subsections (1) and (2)* provide that the Lord Chancellor's duty under section 1(1) does not include a duty to secure that legal aid is provided by the means selected by the individual. For example, in certain cases, the Lord Chancellor may arrange for some services to be provided only by telephone or by other electronic means.

196.   *Subsection (3)* provides that the Lord Chancellor's duty under section 1(1) does not include a duty to secure that legal aid is provided by a person selected by an individual, except as provided in *subsections (4) to (10)*. For example, in civil cases, as at present, the intention is that an individual must select a person with whom the Lord Chancellor has entered into a contract or other arrangement (for example, provision of services by telephone or by other electronic means) for the provision of those services.

197.   In relation to representation for criminal proceedings, *subsection (4) and (5)* provide that an individual may select a legal representative of their own choice and that choice will be respected, subject to regulations made under *subsection (6)*. Those regulations may limit choice in the ways referred to in *subsection (6)*. For example, the regulations may limit the choice to a specified group of providers or may limit the number of legal representatives who can act for any individual at any one time. They may also restrict the right of the individual to appoint a new legal representative in place of one previously chosen.

198.   Similar powers exist in section 15 of the Access to Justice Act 1999 in relation to a right to representation. Under that section provision has been made, for example, limiting an individual's choice to providers who hold a contract with the LSC to provide legal services and about the circumstances in which an individual may be represented by Queen's Counsel or by more than one junior advocate, and limitations have been placed on an individual's right to transfer a representation order to a new provider.

199.   Section 26 does not prevent regulations restricting an individual's choice to a person employed by the Lord Chancellor (unlike section 15(4) of the Access to Justice Act 1999).

Section 28: Position of providers of services
200.   Section 28 makes provision similar to the provisions currently set out at section 22(1), (2) and (3) of the Access to Justice Act 1999.

201.   *Subsection (1)* provides that, unless regulations state otherwise, the provision of legal aid to an individual does not affect the relationship between the individual and the provider of the services, including any lawyer-client privilege.

202.   *Subsection (2)* provides that providers of legal aid may not seek remuneration (or a "top up" payment) from their clients in addition to that provided under the legal aid scheme, unless the Lord Chancellor authorises them to do so.

203.   *Subsection (3)* provides that regulations may allow for a provider to be entitled to be paid for work done up to the time when a determination that a person qualifies for legal aid is withdrawn.

Section 29: Code of conduct

204.   Section 29 makes provision about a code of conduct to be observed by certain types of persons when providing legal aid.

205.   *Subsection (1)* provides that the Lord Chancellor must publish a code of conduct to be followed by civil servants and by employees of any body set up by the Lord Chancellor to provide legal aid, such as a body like the Public Defender Service that has been established by the LSC.

206.   *Subsection (2)* provides that the code is to include the same range of duties currently listed at section 16(2) of the Access to Justice Act 1999, namely duties to avoid discrimination, duties to protect the interests of the individuals for whom services are provided, duties to the courts and tribunals, duties to avoid conflicts of interest, duties of confidentiality and duties to act in accordance with professional rules.

207.   *Subsection (4)* provides that the persons to whom the code applies are not subject to the direction of the Lord Chancellor when they provide services. This is to ensure their independence in providing such services.

Section 30: Position of other parties, courts and tribunals

208.   Section 30 makes provision similar to section 22(4), (5) and (6) of the Access to Justice Act 1999.

209.   *Subsection (1)* provides that unless regulations provide otherwise, the fact that legal aid is provided to an individual does not affect the rights of any third party or the principles governing the exercise of a court's or tribunal's discretion.

210.   *Subsections (2) and (3)* enable regulations to make provision about court or tribunal procedures in cases involving legal aid services.

Supplementary
Section 31 and Schedule 3: Legal aid for legal persons

211.   Section 31 gives effect to Schedule 3.

Schedule 3: Legal aid for legal persons

212.   Schedule 3 provides for the possibility that civil and criminal legal aid may be made available to a legal person, that is a legal entity other than an individual, for example a body corporate. All determinations in relation to legal aid for legal persons will be made by the Director.

213.   *Paragraph 2* defines an exceptional case determination for the purposes of this Schedule. This is the same as an exceptional case determination under section 10(3).

214.   *Paragraph 3(1)* makes provision about when civil legal services are to be made available to a legal person.   First, the Director must have made (and not have withdrawn) an exceptional case determination in relation to the person and the services. Second, the Director must have determined that the person qualifies for the services in accordance with Part 1 of the Act (and not withdrawn that determination). *Paragraph 3(2)* requires the Director to make such a determination in accordance

with the means testing provisions (section 21) and the criteria in regulations made under section 11(1)(b). It also requires a determination that a legal person qualifies for civil legal services to specify the type of service and the matters in relation to which the services are to be available. *Paragraph 3(3)* applies the powers in section 12(2) to (6) to make provision about procedures for the making and withdrawal of determinations.

215. *Paragraph 4(1) and (2)* enables the Lord Chancellor to make regulations enabling prescribed advice and assistance for criminal proceedings to be made available to legal persons who are involved in investigations which may lead to criminal proceedings and to legal persons who are before a court, tribunal or other person in criminal proceedings. In order for such prescribed advice and assistance to be made available, prescribed conditions must be met, the Director must have made (and not withdrawn) an exceptional case determination in relation to the legal person and the proceedings, and the Director must have determined that the legal person qualifies for such advice and assistance in accordance with the regulations (and not withdrawn that determination).

216. The effect of *paragraph 4(3)* is that, when making the regulations, the Lord Chancellor must have regard in particular to the interests of justice and the regulations must require the Director to make determinations having regard in particular to the interests of justice and may require the Director to do so in accordance with the means testing provisions (section 21) and in accordance with criteria set out in the regulations. Paragraph 4(3) also applies provisions in section 15(6) to (9) about procedures for the making and withdrawal of determinations.

217. *Paragraph 5* makes provision about representation for the purposes of criminal proceedings for legal persons. In order for such representation to be made available, the legal person must be a description of legal person specified in relation to those proceedings or the proceedings must involve resisting an appeal to the Crown Court in a private prosecution case. The conditions for representation for criminal proceedings being made available are: *first (paragraph 5(2)(a))*, that the Director has made (and not withdrawn) an exceptional case determination, and *second (paragraph 5(2)(b))*, that the Director has determined (provisionally or otherwise) that the legal person qualifies for representation in accordance with Part 1 of the Act (and has not withdrawn the determination). *Paragraph 5(5)* requires the Director to make an exceptional case determination in accordance with the interests of justice. *Paragraph 5(6)* requires the Director to make the determination that a legal person qualifies for representation in accordance with the means testing provisions (section 21) and in accordance with the interests of justice. *Paragraph 5(12)* provides that the Lord Chancellor may by regulations prescribe the circumstances in which making representation available to a legal person for the purpose of criminal proceedings is to be taken as being in the interests of justice.

218. *Paragraph 5(3)* provides that where a legal person qualifies for representation, that representation will cover any preliminary or incidental proceedings and the effect of *sub-paragraph (4)* is that regulations made by the Lord Chancellor under section 16(4) and (5) about whether proceedings are or are not to be regarded as preliminary

or incidental apply in relation to legal persons unless those regulations provide otherwise.

219.   *Paragraph 5(7)* applies the provisions in section 18(2) to (7) about procedures for the making and withdrawal of determinations made by the Direction under paragraph 5(2).

220.   *Paragraph 5(8)* provides that the Director may not make a provisional determination under *paragraph 5(2)(b)* that the legal person qualifies for representation in accordance with Part 1 of the Act unless regulations made under *paragraph 5(9)* provide for this.

221.   *Paragraph 5(9)* enables the Lord Chancellor to make regulations authorising the Director to make a provisional determination that a legal person qualifies for representation for the purposes of criminal proceedings in the circumstances described in sub-paragraph (9)(a) to (c).   *Paragraph 5(10)* applies *subsections (2) and (3)* of section 20 to regulations made under *paragraph 5(9)*.

222.   *Paragraphs 6, 7 and 8* ensure that the means testing provisions (section 21) and provisions about contributions and costs (section 23, 24, 25 and 26 and Schedule 2) apply for the purposes of determinations about whether a legal person qualifies for legal aid.   *Paragraph 9* ensures that section 27 (choice of provider of services etc), section 28 (position of providers of services), section 29 (code of conduct) and section 30 (position of other parties, courts and tribunals) apply in relation to services that are provided to a legal person under Part 1 of the Act.   *Paragraph 10* ensures that sections 34 (restriction on disclosure of other information), section 35 (exceptions from restrictions under section 34) and section 41 (orders, regulations and directions) apply in the context of legal aid for legal persons as if references to an individual included a legal person.

Section 32: Foreign law
223.   Section 32 concerns the availability of legal aid services in relation to foreign law. This section reflects the current provision about legal aid in relation to foreign law at section 19 of the Access to Justice Act 1999.

224.   *Subsection (1)* restricts the applicability of the civil legal services made available under the Act to the law of England and Wales only, except where the Act specifies otherwise, where foreign law is relevant to proceedings in England and Wales, or where the Lord Chancellor specifies otherwise by order. *Subsection (2)* makes similar provision in relation to criminal legal aid.

225.   *Subsection (3)* limits the Lord Chancellor's ability to make an order under *subsections (1) and (2)*.

Section 33: Restriction on disclosure of information about financial resources
226.   Section 33 provides for the protection of information obtained under the information gateway in section 22.   It makes provision similar to the provision in paragraphs 6 to 8 of Schedule 3 to the Access to Justice Act 1999.

227.   *Subsections (1) and (2)* provide that a person who receives information under section 22 or under this section may only disclose or use that information if it is necessary or expedient to do so in connection with determining financial eligibility for legal aid.

228.   *Subsection (3)* qualifies *subsection (2)* by providing for limited circumstances in which the information may be used for purposes other than assessing financial eligibility. Disclosure is permitted if it would be in accordance with an enactment or in accordance with a court order, if it is for the purposes of the investigation or prosecution of an offence or suspected offence or if it is for the purposes of proceedings before a court, including instituting such proceedings. Disclosure is also permitted if the information has already been lawfully disclosed to the public.

229.   *Subsection (4)* provides that disclosure or use of information contrary to this section is a criminal offence and specifies the maximum penalties. The penalty for the offence on conviction on indictment will be imprisonment for a term not exceeding two years or a fine (or both). The penalty for the offence on summary conviction, in England and Wales, will be imprisonment for a term not exceeding 12 months or a fine not exceeding the statutory maximum (currently £,5000) (or both) and, in Northern Ireland, will be imprisonment for a term not exceeding 6 months or a fine not exceeding the statutory maximum (or both). *Subsection (7)* provides in relation to the summary penalty in England and Wales that for an offence committed before the commencement of section 154(1) of the 2003 Act the reference in *subsection (4)(b)(i)* to 12 months has effect as if it were a reference to 6 months.

230.   *Subsection (5)* provides a statutory defence to the criminal offence detailed in *subsection (4)* where the person charged with the offence reasonably believed that the disclosure or use was lawful.

Section 34: Restriction on disclosure of other information
231.   Section 34 provides for the protection of information other than information to which section 33 applies (see *subsection (7)*) which is given to the Lord Chancellor, the Director, a court, tribunal or any other person or body which has functions under Part 1 of this Act.

232.   *Subsection (1)* describes the information to which the provisions apply: information provided to the persons referred to in the paragraph above in connection with an individual applying for or in receipt of legal aid.

233.   Subject to the exceptions in section 35, *subsection (2)* prevents such information from being disclosed. *Subsection (3)* makes disclosure contrary to this section a criminal offence and sets out the maximum penalties for that offence. The penalty for the offence will be, on summary conviction, a fine not exceeding level 4 on the standard scale, which is currently £2,500.

234.   *Subsection (4)* provides a statutory defence for a person charged with the offence where they reasonably believed that the disclosure was lawful.

235.   *Subsection (5)* requires the consent of the Director of Public Prosecutions before proceedings can be brought in relation to an alleged breach of this section.

236.   *Subsection (6)* provides that section 34 does not apply to information provided to a provider of services by or on behalf of an individual for whom the services are, or would be, provided under Part 1 of the Act.

Section 35: Exceptions from restriction under section 34

237.   Section 35 provides for exceptions to the bar on disclosure in *subsection (2)* of section 34.

238.   *Subsection (1)* provides for a general exception relating to the disclosure of information for the purpose of enabling or assisting the Lord Chancellor or the Secretary of State for Justice in carrying out their functions. It is not limited to functions created by statute. This subsection also provides for similar exceptions where the Director or a court, tribunal or other person is carrying out functions under Part 1 of the Act, as well as in connection with any proceedings involving services delivered under Part 1.

239.   *Subsection (2)* provides for an exception relating to disclosure of information where disclosure would be in accordance with the law of England and Wales, as well as when ordered by a court or for the purposes of court proceedings. This subsection also creates an exception relating to disclosure of information for the purposes of proceedings before a court, including instituting such proceedings, for the purpose of a criminal investigation and for the purpose of allowing a tribunal to properly exercise its disciplinary functions.   This subsection also provides an exception where information has previously been lawfully disclosed to the public.

240.   *Subsection (3)* provides two further exceptions to the restriction on disclosure. The first exception is where information is to be released in a form in which information pertaining to the individual cannot be identified. The second exception is where the information requested relates to any grant, loan or other payment made by the Lord Chancellor pursuant to functions under Part 1 of the Act.

241.   *Subsection (4)* provides an exception where an individual consents to the release of information pertaining to them. *Subsection (4)* also provides that if the information was provided by someone other than the individual to whom it relates the person who provided the information must also consent to its disclosure.

242.   *Subsections (5) and (6)* ensure that disclosure of information covered by section 33 is not prevented by that section, provided that the restricted period of 100 years has passed, that disclosure is made by a person who is a public authority for the purposes of the Freedom of Information Act 2000, and that the information is not held on behalf of another person.

Section 36: Misrepresentation

243.   Section 36 provides criminal penalties for people who intentionally fail to comply with requirements to provide documents or information under Part 1 of the Act, and for people who make a statement or representation which they know or believe to be false when providing documents and information in accordance with Part 1 of the Act. The section largely replicates equivalent provisions in section 21 of the Access to Justice Act 1999. A person found guilty of an offence under this section is liable on

summary conviction to a fine not exceeding level 4 on the standard scale, which is currently £2,500. Unlike the offence under section 21 of the Access to Justice Act 1999, the offence under this section is not punishable by imprisonment.

244.   This section also enables the Lord Chancellor to take proceedings in the county courts to recover losses arising as a result of the failure of an individual to provide documents or information or as the result of a false statement or false representation as required under Part 1 of the Act.

Section 37: Status of the Director and Lord Chancellor

245.   Section 37 makes provision to provide clarity on the status of both the Director and the Lord Chancellor when exercising specific functions.

246.   Section 4(1) of the Act requires the Lord Chancellor to designate a civil servant as the Director.

247.   *Subsection (1)* of section 37 ensures that the Director is to carry out the functions of the statutory office on behalf of the Crown and *subsection (2)* ensures that service as the Director is in the civil service of the State.

248.   *Subsection (3)* provides that the Lord Chancellor is to be treated as a corporation sole for purposes relating to property (and interests in property) under Part 1 of the Act, and for all other purposes relating to the Lord Chancellor's functions in connection with legal aid and other functions under Part 1. This clarifies the position in relation to the Lord Chancellor's ability to hold an interest in land for these purposes and so applies to those charges (statutory or otherwise) which transfer from the LSC to the Lord Chancellor pursuant to Schedule 4 to the Act and those statutory charges that will arise pursuant to section 25 of the Act.

249.   *Subsection (4)* confers on the Lord Chancellor a statutory power to authorise persons to execute instruments conveying property and interests in property held by the Lord Chancellor in connection with legal aid or other functions under Part 1.

250.   *Subsection (5)* provides that such an instrument executed by or on behalf of the Lord Chancellor is to be received in evidence and, unless the contrary is proved, to be treated as having been so executed.

Section 38: Abolition of Legal Services Commission

251.   Section 38 abolishes the LSC. The LSC was established under section 1(1) of the Access to Justice Act 1999. Following the transfer of legal aid functions to the Lord Chancellor under section 1, it is intended that an Executive Agency will be created within the Ministry of Justice to administer legal aid.

252.   *Subsections (3) and (4)* set out provisions for the production of a report and statement of accounts for the final period up to the day before the LSC ceases to exist.

Schedule 4: Transfer of employees and property etc of Legal Services Commission

253.   Schedule 4 provides for employees of the LSC to become civil servants and for the transfer of property, assets and liabilities held in the name of the LSC to the Lord Chancellor or to the Secretary of State.

254.   LSC employees are currently public sector employees rather than civil servants. *Paragraph 1* of Schedule 4 provides that, when the new arrangements for legal aid come into force, LSC employees become civil servants on their existing terms and conditions (save as to pensions and severance). It makes provision to ensure that the transfer does not break the continuity of their employment.

255.   *Paragraph 4* enables the Lord Chancellor to make a scheme transferring the LSC's rights and liabilities in respect of occupational pension schemes or compensation schemes to the Lord Chancellor or the Secretary of State.

256.   *Subparagraph (7)* provides that a transfer scheme may apply legislation relating to compensation schemes and occupational schemes with modifications, so far as is necessary for giving effect to the scheme.

257.   *Subparagraph (8)* provides that the transfer scheme may amend or otherwise modify a compensation scheme.

258.   When employees of the LSC become civil servants there will be no active members of the (currently two) LSC occupational pension schemes. *Paragraph 5* provides the Lord Chancellor with a power to make a scheme to merge the LSC occupational pension schemes. The power includes provision for the winding up of an LSC occupational pension scheme. A merger must not to any extent deprive members of the LSC occupational pension schemes, or other beneficiaries under those schemes, of rights accrued before the merger takes effect.

259.   *Paragraph 6* transfers interests in land held in the name of the LSC to the Secretary of State for Communities and Local Government who holds freeholds and leaseholds on behalf of other government departments. Charges on land are specifically excluded from this paragraph because those charges on property in connection with civil proceedings are to transfer to the Lord Chancellor pursuant to paragraph 7.

260.   *Paragraph 7* transfers other property, rights, powers, duties and liabilities of the LSC to the Lord Chancellor. Therefore, for example, by operation of law, contracts (in the name of the LSC) are novated to the Lord Chancellor, including contracts made for the provision of legal aid services.

261.   *Paragraph 11* allows the Lord Chancellor to make by statutory instrument, consequential, supplementary, incidental, transitional, transitory or saving provision in connection with the transfers effected by Schedule 4 or schemes made under Schedule 4.

Section 39 and Schedule 5: Consequential amendments

262.   *Subsection (1)* provides that Schedule 5 of the Bill has effect. Schedule 5 makes various amendments and repeals which are consequential on the changes to legal aid made by Part 1. There are, for example, a number of amendments to delete references to the LSC in other legislation, such as in Schedule 1 to the Public Records Act 1958 (paragraph 1 of Schedule 5) and in Schedule 2 to the Parliamentary Commissioner Act 1967 (paragraph 2 of Schedule 5). There are also, for example, a number of amendments to replace references to the Community Legal Service and the Criminal Defence Service, such as in the Solicitors Act 1974 (paragraphs 7 to 9 of Schedule 5) and in the Prosecution of Offences Act 1985 (paragraphs 22 to 25 of Schedule 5).

263.   *Subsections (2) to (10)* ensure that the Lord Chancellor is able abolish the LSC in advance of some or all of the provisions of Part 1 of the Bill being brought into force.

264.   *Subsection (2)* gives the Lord Chancellor the power, where the Lord Chancellor considers it appropriate as part of the arrangements for moving from the legal aid arrangements under the Access to Justice Act 1999 to the operation of the legal aid arrangements under Part 1 of this Act, to make regulations requiring or enabling prescribed services that immediately before the date of such regulations may be funded under the Access to Justice Act, to be made available under Part 1 of this Act for a temporary period specified or described in the regulations.

265.   *Subsection (4)* provides the Lord Chancellor with the power, where the Lord Chancellor considers it appropriate for the LSC to cease to exist before Part 1 of this Act is brought into force, to make regulations making provision for the Lord Chancellor and the Director, or persons authorised by them, to carry out functions of the LSC under Part 1 of the Access to Justice Act for a temporary period specified or described in the regulations. *Subsection (6)* provides that regulations under *subsection (4)* may not provide for the Lord Chancellor to take decisions about whether services should be funded in individual cases and regulations may not provide for the Lord Chancellor to give directions or guidance about the carrying out of functions under Part 1 of the Access to Justice Act 1999 in relation to individual cases.

266.   *Subsection (7)* provides that regulations under section 39 may amend, appeal, revoke or otherwise modify Part 1 of the Access to Justice Act, Part 1 of this Act, or any other Act or instrument made under an Act, and that a temporary period described by such regulations may be described, in particular, by reference to the coming into force of a provision of this Act or the repeal of a provision of Part 1 of the Access to Justice Act 1999.

267.   Any regulations made under section 39 that amend or repeal a provision of an Act are subject to the affirmative procedure unless they revoke such regulations or insert or repeal provision previously repealed or inserted by such regulations, in which case they would be subject to the negative procedure (see section 41(7)(k)).

Section 40 and Schedule 6: Northern Ireland: information about financial resources

268. Section 40 and Schedule 6 provide a gateway for the disclosure of information to the chief executive of the Northern Ireland Legal Services Commission (or other prescribed person) by the Secretary of State (in practice, the Secretary of State for Work and Pensions), the Commissioners for Her Majesty's Revenue and Customs ("the Commissioners"), the Department for Social Development in Northern Ireland or the Department of Finance and Personnel in Northern Ireland (the "relevant Northern Ireland Departments"). It also provides restrictions on the disclosure of that information. These provisions closely mirror the provisions in sections 22 and 33 that relate to information requests by the Director (or other prescribed persons).

269. *Paragraph 1(1)* of Schedule 6 enables the chief executive (or other prescribed person) to make a request for certain information to the Secretary of State, a relevant Northern Ireland Department or the Commissioners. *Paragraph 1(2)* provides that such a request may only be made for the purpose of facilitating a determination about an individual's financially eligibility for legal aid under the Northern Ireland legislation that governs the provision of legal aid.

270. *Paragraph 1(3)* lists the categories of information which may be requested from the Secretary of State or the relevant Northern Ireland Departments. It includes a power to add further categories of information by secondary legislation.

271. *Paragraph 1(4)* lists the categories of information which may be requested from the Commissioners. It includes a power to add further categories of information by secondary legislation, with the Commissioners' consent (see *paragraph 1(6)*).

272. *Paragraph 1(7)* provides that the Secretary of State, the relevant Northern Ireland Departments and the Commissioners may disclose to the chief executive (or other prescribed person) information specified in an information request made under this Schedule.

273. *Paragraph 2* of Schedule 6 provides for the protection of information obtained under the information gateway in paragraph 1. *Paragraph 2(1) and (2)* provide that a person who receives information under paragraph 1 of this Schedule may only disclose or use that information if it is necessary or expedient to do so in connection with determining financial eligibility for legal aid.

274. *Paragraph 2(3)* qualifies *paragraph 2(2)* by providing for limited circumstances in which the information may be used for purposes other than assessing financial eligibility. Disclosure is permitted if it would be in accordance with an enactment or in accordance with a court order, if it is for the purposes of the investigation or prosecution of an offence or suspected offence or if it for the purposes of proceedings before a court, including instituting such proceedings. Disclosure is also permitted if the information has already been lawfully disclosed to the public.

275. *Paragraph 2(4)* provides that disclosure or use of information contrary to this section is a criminal offence and specifies the maximum penalties. The penalty for the offence will be, on conviction on indictment, imprisonment for a term not exceeding two years or a fine (or both) and, on summary conviction in England and Wales,

imprisonment for a term not exceeding 12 months or a fine not exceeding the statutory maximum (or both), and in Northern Ireland to imprisonment for a term not exceeding 6 months or a fine not exceeding the statutory maximum (currently £5,000), or both.

276.   *Paragraph 2(5)* provides a statutory defence to the criminal offence detailed in *paragraph 2(4)* where the person charged with the offence reasonably believed that the disclosure or use was lawful.

277.   *Paragraph 2(7)* clarifies, in relation to the summary penalty in England and Wales for an offence under this paragraph committed before the commencement of section 154(1) of the 2003 Act, that the reference to 12 months imprisonment has effect as if it were a reference to 6 months.

278.   *Paragraph 3* of Schedule 6 enables the Department for Justice in Northern Ireland to make consequential, supplementary, incidental or transitional provision by regulations in relation to the provisions of this Schedule. *Paragraph 4* makes provision about the powers to make regulations under the Schedule. Those powers are conferred on the Department for Justice in Northern Ireland. Under *paragraph 4(4)* the first regulations under paragraph 1 and any regulations under paragraph 3 that amend or repeal Northern Ireland legislation will be subject to the affirmative resolution procedure but otherwise regulations under the Schedule are subject to the negative resolution procedure.

Section 41: Orders, regulations and directions
279.   *Subsections (1) to (3)* of section 41 make further provision about the exercise of powers under Part 1 to make orders, regulations and directions. For example, they provide that such instruments may make different provision for different geographic areas and that they may make transitory provision. They may also make different provision for the purpose of proceedings before different courts and tribunals, for particular classes of individual or for individuals selected by reference to particular criteria or on a sampling basis. This provides flexibility and will enable provisions to be piloted. *Subsections (4) to (11)* concern the Parliamentary procedure which applies to secondary legislation under Part 1 of the Bill, including the procedure which applies where the Lord Chancellor makes an urgency statement in respect of regulations made under section 11(1)(b) (criteria for qualifying for civil legal aid).

Section 42: Interpretation
280.   Section 42 provides definitions of terms used in Part 1.

Part 2: Litigation funding and costs
Payments for legal services in civil cases
Section 44: Conditional fee agreements: success fees
281.   A conditional fee agreement ("CFA") is a private funding agreement between a lawyer and a client under which the lawyer agrees to represent the client on a 'no win, no fee' basis. Under the agreement, the lawyer does not generally receive a fee from

the client if the case is lost[11]. However, if the case is won, the lawyers' costs (the 'base costs') are generally recoverable from the losing party. In these cases, the lawyer can charge an uplift on these base costs, which is currently recoverable from the losing party. This uplift is known as the 'success fee'. The maximum success fee that may be charged under a CFA is prescribed by secondary legislation. In all cases, the current maximum uplift that may be charged is 100% of the base costs.

282.   Section 44 amends sections 58 and 58A of the Courts and Legal Services Act 1990, which currently make provision as regards the regulation of CFAs and the recoverability of success fees. The effect of the amendments is that a success fee under a CFA will no longer be recovered from a losing party in any proceedings. A lawyer will still be able to recover a success fee from a client under a CFA, but how it is to be calculated in certain proceedings will now be subject to further regulation.

283.   *Subsection (2)* inserts new subsections (4A) and (4B) into section 58. New subsection (4A) provides that CFAs which provide for a success fee and relate to proceedings prescribed by the Lord Chancellor must comply with certain additional conditions in order to be enforceable. New subsection (4B) sets out those conditions. They require the CFA to cap the success fee at a percentage of certain damages awarded to the client if they win. The cap and the kinds of damages to which it applies are to be prescribed by the Lord Chancellor. These provisions will be of particular importance in personal injury claims, for example, where it is proposed to exclude damages for future care and loss from the calculation of any success fee.

284.   By virtue of *subsection (5)*, orders made under new subsections (4A) and (4B) of section 58 will be subject to the affirmative resolution procedure.

285.   *Subsection (3)* amends subsection (5) of section 58A, the effect of which is to require the Lord Chancellor to consult with designated judges, the General Council of the Bar, the Law Society and such other bodies as he considers appropriate before making an order under new subsections (4A) and (4B).

286.   *Subsection (4)* inserts a new subsection (6) into section 58A, the effect of which is to prevent the recoverability of a success fee from a losing party under a court's costs order.

287.   *Subsection (6)* contains a saving. It provides that a costs order made in proceedings about a matter may continue to provide for the recovery of a success fee from the losing party where the success fee is payable under a CFA entered into for the purposes of that matter before the day on which section 44(4) comes into force or where it is payable under a collective CFA under which advocacy or litigation services were provided to a person in respect of that matter before that day.

---

[11] A CFA can also be arranged on a 'no win, low fee' basis.

Section 45: Damages-based agreements

288.   Damages-based agreements ("DBAs") are another type of 'no win, no fee' agreement under which a lawyer can recover a percentage of the client's damages if the case is won, but will receive nothing if the case is lost. Currently, solicitors and barristers are not permitted to act under DBAs in civil litigation, but solicitors are permitted to act under DBAs in non-contentious business, including cases before employment tribunals.

289.   Section 45 amends section 58AA of the Courts and Legal Services Act 1990 (inserted by section 154 of the Coroners and Justice Act 2009), which currently provides that DBAs are enforceable only when they relate to employment matters. The effect of the amendments is to enable the use of DBAs in most civil litigation by persons providing advocacy services, litigation services or claims management services.

290.   *Subsections (2) and (3)* omit references to employment matters, the effect of which is that a DBA need not relate to an employment matter in order to be enforceable.

291.   *Subsection (5)* inserts new paragraph (aa) into subsection (4) of section 58AA, to provide that a DBA may not relate to proceedings which may not be the subject of an enforceable CFA under section 58A of the Courts and Legal Services Act 1990 (essentially criminal and family proceedings) or to proceedings of a description prescribed by the Lord Chancellor.

292.   Section 58AA(4) also sets out other conditions that must be met for a DBA to be enforceable. The amendments made by *subsections (6) and (7)* of this section make clear that the Lord Chancellor may, but need not, prescribe the information which a legal representative must provide to a claimant prior to entering a DBA and the maximum amount which may be paid under the DBA from the claimant's damages. Any regulations made under section 58AA(4) are subject to the affirmative resolution procedure (see *subsection (12)*).

293.   *Subsection (8)* amends section 58AA to provide that rules of court may be made in respect of the assessment of costs in proceedings funded under DBAs. For the avoidance of doubt, *subsection (9)* inserts a definition of "proceedings" into section 58AA, which includes any sort of proceedings for resolving disputes (and not just proceedings in a court), whether commenced or contemplated.

294.   *Subsection (10)* further amends section 58AA to provide that, except where they relate to employment matters, non-contentious business agreements between solicitors and clients to which section 57 of the Solicitors Act 1974 applies will not be unenforceable by reason of the provisions of section 58AA.

Section 46: Recovery of insurance premiums by way of costs

295.   After the Event ("ATE") insurance can be taken out by parties in a CFA-funded case to insure against the risk of having to pay their opponent's costs and their own disbursements if they lose. Under the current arrangements, ATE insurance premiums are recoverable from the losing party. Currently, the recovery of such insurance premiums by way of costs is provided for by section 29 of the Access to Justice Act 1999.

296.   Section 46 repeals section 29 and makes new provision relating to the recoverability of insurance premiums from a losing party. The effect of the new provision is to provide that the cost of any insurance policy taken out by a party to insure against the risk of having to pay their opponent's costs and their own disbursements if they lose cannot be recovered from a losing party except in certain limited circumstances.

297.   *Subsection (1)* inserts a new section 58C into the Courts and Legal Services Act 1990. The effect of section 58C is to limit the recoverability of insurance premiums to certain clinical negligence proceedings and only allow recovery of the premium to the extent that it relates to the costs of an expert report or reports (section 58C(1) and (2)). This exception reflects concerns that expert reports in clinical negligence cases can often be very expensive. New section 58C enables the Lord Chancellor to make regulations to prescribe the circumstances in which the premium would be recoverable and the amount of the premium that may be recovered. The maximum amount may, in particular, be prescribed by specifying a percentage of the relevant part of the premium or an amount calculated in a prescribed manner (section 58C(4)).

Section 47: Recovery where body undertakes to meet costs liabilities

298.   Certain bodies, such as trade unions and other membership organisations, often provide legal services to their members as a benefit of membership. Section 30 of the Access to Justice Act 1999 allows bodies that are approved by the Lord Chancellor to recover from a losing party the cost of insuring themselves against the risk of paying costs to another party in the event of losing a claim. The effect of section 46 is to prevent the recovery of these insurance premiums from a losing party.

299.   *Subsection (1)* repeals section 30 of the Access to Justice Act 1999. Although similar in effect to section 48, section 49 does not provide for any exceptions to non-recoverability, since the circumstances which require specific provisions relating to expert reports in clinical negligence cases do not arise.

300.   *Subsection (2)* contains a saving. It provides that a costs order made in favour of a member of a body in proceedings about a matter may provide for the recovery of a body's costs where the body gave a specific undertaking to the member to meet the costs of other parties to proceedings about that matter before the day on which section 47 comes into force.

Section 48: Sections 44 and 46 and diffuse mesothelioma proceedings

301.   Section 48 provides that sections 44 (abolition of recoverability of success fees) and 46 (abolition of recoverability of "ATE" insurance premiums) may not be commenced in respect of proceedings relating to claims for damages for diffuse mesothelioma until the Lord Chancellor has reviewed the likely impact of those sections on such claims and has published a report on the review's conclusions. This means that, until that time, successful claimants in these cases will continue to be able to recover success fees and ATE insurance premiums from losing defendants.

302.   Diffuse mesothelioma is defined by reference to the Pneumoconiosis etc (Workers' Compensation) Act 1979[12].

Section 49: Divorce etc proceedings: orders for payment in respect of legal services

303.   Part II of the Matrimonial Causes Act 1973 ("the 1973 Act") makes provision (mirrored for civil partnerships by Schedule 5 to the Civil Partnership Act 2004 ("the 2004 Act")) for the court's powers to make orders "for the purpose of adjusting the financial position of the parties to a marriage and any children of the family in connection with proceedings for divorce, nullity of marriage or judicial separation". The orders include orders that one party to the marriage makes periodical payments to the other or for a child of the family; or that one party pays a lump sum to the other or for a child of the family. It is not possible to make an *interim* order for a lump sum, or periodical payments, by one party to the marriage to the other. Section 22, however, makes provision for *maintenance pending suit*, where the court may at any time in the proceedings make an order for one party to make to the other "such periodical payments for his or her maintenance … as the court thinks reasonable", and case law has developed in which the court has included an element to enable that other party to fund that party's costs of pursuing the proceedings where he or she has insufficient immediately available resources to do so.[13]

304.   Section 49 amends the 1973 Act to confer a more general power, not limited to maintenance pending suit, for a court in divorce, nullity of marriage or judicial separation proceedings to order payment by one party to the other for the purpose of securing legal services.

305.   *Subsection (1)* amends section 22 of the 1973 Act to provide that the court cannot use its existing powers to use maintenance pending suit to cover payment for legal services, so that such payment will be covered by the new power alone.

306.   *Subsection (2)* inserts into the 1973 Act a new section 22ZA, which sets out the court's power and the conditions for its exercise as well as the terms on which any order may be made. Subsections (1) and (2) of the new section make provision about the scope of the power and its purpose: the power may be exercised in proceedings for divorce, nullity of marriage or judicial separation (including ancillary relief proceedings), and is a power to make an order requiring one party to pay to the other (referred to as the applicant) an amount to enable the other to obtain legal services for the purposes of the proceedings.

307.   Subsection (3) of the new section contains the test for making an order, which requires the court to be satisfied that without this money the applicant would not otherwise reasonably be able to obtain appropriate legal services for the purposes of the proceedings or any part of them. This, by virtue of subsection (4) of the new section, includes being satisfied that the applicant could not obtain a loan or secure

---

[12] 1979 c.41

[13] The leading case, which gives the history of the development of the case law in this respect and restates the principles governing the making of such orders, is the Court of Appeal case of *Currey v Currey* [2006] EWCA Civ 1338

legal services with the promise of payment on conclusion of the proceedings and division of the assets.

308.   Subsection (5) of the new section provides for flexibility in making an order. The court does not have to assess the likely need for legal services for the entire proceedings and make an order for a payment to cover that (although that is possible), but may order payment to cover specified services, services in a specified period or for a specified part of the proceedings, or a combination ("specified" being explained in subsection (11) of the new section as meaning specified by the court). Coupled with the ability to make more than one order, this enables the court, for example, to make an order for payment for services limited to addressing a specific issue or issues in the proceedings at an initial stage and to review the position at the conclusion of that stage.

309.   Subsections (6) to (8) of the new section provide for additional flexibility, enabling the court to order payment to be made in instalments or for it (or any part of it) to be deferred, and to vary an order if there has been a material change of circumstances. Subsection (9) of the new section provides for the paying party to have credit for a payment made pursuant to an order under the section in that the amount paid will be set off, in the event of an order for costs as between the parties, against any costs which the applicant might be able to recover.

310.   Subsection (10) of the new section defines "legal services" in a broad and flexible way which will cover disbursements as well as pure legal advice, so that, for example, if the court were satisfied that an initial report was necessary, it could order payment of an appropriate amount to cover the cost of that report as part of the legal services.

Section 50: Divorce etc proceedings: matters to be considered by court making legal services order

311.   Section 50 inserts into the 1973 Act a new section 22ZB, which provides for the matters the court must consider when deciding whether to make (or vary) an order under the new section 22ZA and the terms of any order so made or varied.

312.   Subsection (1) of the new section 22ZB lists the matters to which the court must have regard. These include the overall financial position of both parties (as to which subsection (2) of the new section makes supplementary provision about the meaning of "earning capacity" of a party), what the main proceedings are about, whether the party who is being asked to pay already has legal representation, the behaviour of the applicant in the proceedings and the extent to which the party who is being asked to pay is reasonably able to do so (as to which subsection (3) of the new section requires the court to have regard in particular to whether the order is likely to cause undue hardship to the paying party, or to prevent the paying party from obtaining legal services for the purposes of the proceedings).

313.   Subsection (4) of the new section provides for the Lord Chancellor to have power to amend the list of factors in subsection (1), and subsections (5) and (6) require such amendment to be by way of statutory instrument subject to affirmative resolution procedure. Subsection (7) of the new section provides for the term "legal services" in this new section to have the same meaning as in the new section 22ZA.

Section 51: Divorce etc proceedings: orders for sale of property

314. Section 51 amends section 24A of the Matrimonial Causes Act 1973 so that the court's power to order the sale of property in order to give effect to certain types of order extends also to the new type of order under the new section 22ZA. 'Property' could be assets such as a holiday home, shares or other illiquid assets.

Section 52: Dissolution etc proceedings: orders for payment in respect of legal services
Section 53: Dissolution etc proceedings: matters to be considered by court making legal services order
Section 54: Dissolution etc proceedings: orders for sale of property

315. Sections 52 to 54 make provision in respect of civil partnership proceedings which mirrors that in sections 49 to 51.

Offers to settle
Section 55: Payment of additional amount to successful claimant

316. The costs sanctions against a defendant for failing to accept a claimant's offer to settle generally amount to considerably less than the sanctions against a claimant for failing to beat a defendant's offer to settle. Consequently, there is less incentive for a defendant to accept a reasonable offer from the claimant than for a claimant to accept a reasonable offer by the defendant.

317. Section 55 enables rules of court to be made in relation to cases involving a claim for money which permit a court to order an additional amount to be paid to a claimant by a defendant who does not accept a claimant's offer to settle where the court gives judgement for the claimant that is at least as advantageous as an offer the claimant made to settle the claim. It also confers power by order to provide that rules of court may provide that in non-monetary claims a defendant may be required to pay an amount to a claimant where the court gives judgment in favour of the claimant which is at least as advantageous as an offer the claimant made to settle the claim. These provisions will be in addition to the current sanctions that the court may order and which are available under Part 36 of the Civil Procedure Rules (namely the payment of interest on damages, interest on costs and the payment of costs on an indemnity rather than a standard basis).

318. *Subsection (1)* makes provision for rules of court to be made in respect of monetary claims so that courts may order a defendant to pay an additional sum to a claimant where the court awards the claimant a benefit the value of which is at least as advantageous as an offer the claimant made to settle the claim, which the claimant has made in accordance with Part 36 of the Civil Procedure Rules. *Subsection (2)* provides that rules made under *subsection (1)* may include provision as to the assessment of whether a judgment is at least as advantageous as an offer to settle.

319. The effect of *subsection (3)* is to enable the Lord Chancellor to prescribe, as a percentage of the value of the benefit awarded to the claimant, the maximum additional sum that the court may order. The Lord Chancellor may prescribe different percentage values for different values of claim (by virtue of *subsection (10)*).

320. *Subsection (4)* enables the Lord Chancellor to provide, by order, that rules of court may be made to enable a court to make an order in non-monetary claims (or mixed non-monetary and monetary claims) requiring a defendant to pay an amount to a claimant where the court gives judgment in favour of the claimant which is at least as advantageous as an offer the claimant made to settle the claim.

321. *Subsection (5)* provides that in claims to which *subsection (4)* applies, an order made by the Lord Chancellor must provide for the amount payable to be calculated in one or more of three specified ways, namely by reference to costs ordered to be paid to the claimant, or any amount of money that is awarded to the claimant in the proceedings, or the value of any non-monetary benefit awarded to the claimant.

322. *Subsection (6)* additionally requires that any order made under *subsection (4)* must provide that rules of court made under the order may include provision as to the assessment of whether a judgment is at least as advantageous as an offer to settle, and may provide that such rules may make provision as to the calculation of the value of any non-monetary benefit awarded to a claimant.

323. *Subsection (7)* provides that conditions prescribed by the Lord Chancellor which must be satisfied before an additional amount can be ordered to be paid may, in particular, relate to the nature of the claim, the amount of money awarded to the claimant and the value of the non-monetary benefit awarded to the claimant. The effect of *subsections (8) and (9)* is that any order made by the Lord Chancellor under this section must be made by statutory instrument subject to the negative resolution procedure.

324. *Subsection (10)* provides that rules of court made under section 55 may make different provision in relation to different cases.

325. *Subsection (11)* defines "civil proceedings", for the purposes of this section as proceedings to which rules of court made under the Civil Procedure Act 1997 apply.

Referral fees
Section 56: Rules against referral fees

326. Section 56 prohibits the payment and receipt by "regulated persons" of referral fees in respect of claims for personal injury and death. In particular, section 56 makes provision to prevent the prohibition on the payment of referral fees in personal injury cases being avoided by presenting the referral fee as a payment for the referral of a connected claim (for example, in a road traffic accident, a credit hire claim or a claim for damage to other property), irrespective of when the referral of information relating to that connected claim occurs. "Regulated person" is defined in section 60 and includes claims management companies ("CMC"s), barristers and solicitors, as well as descriptions of authorised persons under the Financial Services and Markets Act 2000 (such as insurers) if specified in regulations by the Treasury. The prohibition extends to the receipt of a referral fee by a regulated person from a party who, although not a regulated person, provides services to the regulated person's client in connection with their claim, for example a doctor who provides a medical report at the request of a solicitor and who pays the solicitor a fee for the referral. It also enables the Lord Chancellor to make regulations to extend the ban to other types of claim and legal services (defined in *subsection (6)*).

327.   As regards the meaning of "referral", the effect of *subsection (5)* is to treat a referral as the provision by a person other than the client of information that a regulated person authorised to provide legal services would need to make an offer to the client to provide legal services.

328.   *Subsection (8)* provides that a referral fee can be any form of consideration (which could, depending on the circumstances, include, for example, an offer by a solicitor to take on other work at a reduced rate or for no payment at all), other than normal hospitality, whether paid to the referrer directly or to a third party.

Section 57: Effect of rules against referral fees

329.   Section 57 requires relevant regulators to have arrangements in place to monitor and enforce the prohibition on the payment or receipt of referral fees. It also permits regulators to make rules and to use existing powers to enable them to monitor and enforce the prohibition. Under this section, some payments by or to a regulated person may be treated as a referral fee, unless the regulated person can show that the payment was for the provision of a particular service or another reason, and not for the referral – this might include, for example, the payment by a solicitor to a CMC for the obtaining of a medical report prior to the referral of a claim. The Lord Chancellor may make regulations specifying the maximum amount that can be paid for certain services, above which a regulated person will be required to show that the payment is not, or does not include, the payment of a referral fee.

330.   The provisions in section 57 referred to above do not apply where the Financial Services Authority (FSA), which is responsible for the regulation of insurers, and in respect of whom section 58 makes similar provision, is the relevant regulator. However, *subsection (5)*, which provides that a breach of the prohibition does not make a person guilty of an offence and does not give rise to a right of action for breach of statutory duty, and *subsection (6)*, which provides that a contract to make or pay for a referral or arrangement in breach of the prohibition is unenforceable, apply to all regulated persons.

Section 58: Regulation by FSA

331.   Section 58 enables the Treasury to make regulations which will enable the Financial Services Authority to monitor and enforce the prohibition on payment and receipt of referral fees in respect of those it regulates. As section 57 allows regulators to use existing powers to enforce the prohibition, so section 58 allows the Treasury to make regulations enabling the FSA to use existing provisions in the Financial Services and Markets Act 2000[14] for the same purpose. In addition, the regulations may make provisions similar to those under section 57 which require regulated persons to show that a particular payment is not a referral fee and to specify maximum amounts that can be paid for certain services, above which a regulated person will be required to show that the payment is not, or does not include, the payment of a referral fee.

---

[14] 2000 c.8

Section 59: Regulators and regulated persons

332.   Section 59 lists both the "regulators" who are required to monitor and enforce the prohibition on the payment and receipt of referral fees in respect of personal injury claims (namely the FSA, the Claims Management Regulator (CMR), the General Council of the Bar and the Law Society or any other regulatory body specified in regulations by the Lord Chancellor) and the "regulated persons" who are subject to the prohibition (namely CMCs, barristers and solicitors, and insurers (see the note to section 58 above) and any person specified by the Lord Chancellor).

333.   In addition, in respect of any other type of claim or the provision of legal services to which the prohibition might be extended by regulations under section 56(4)(c), section 59, *at subsection (2)*, lists those regulators who could be required to monitor and enforce the prohibition. Again the relevant regulators include both the FSA and the CMR, but *subsection (2)* also recognises that, in extending the prohibition, other providers of legal services, who are required to be regulated by other regulatory bodies, may be brought within the prohibition. The subsection has been drafted to ensure that all potential regulated persons and regulators, who are, in fact, identified in Part 3 of the Legal Services Act 2007[15], can be made subject to the provisions in sections 56 and 57 should the need arise. Further, *subsection (2)* ensures that Alternative Business Structures (see Part 5 of that Act) can also be specified, by the Lord Chancellor, as regulated persons and be made subject to the prohibition as and when it becomes necessary to do so.

Section 60: Referral fees: regulations

334.   Section 60 provides that any regulations made under sections 56 to 59 will be made by statutory instrument, subject to the affirmative procedure.

Pro bono representation

Section 61: Payments in respect of pro bono representation before the Supreme Court

335.   Section 61 amends section 194 of the Legal Services Act 2007. The effect of the amendment will be to enable the Supreme Court to make an order for costs in those cases where a successful party is represented pro bono (i.e. free of charge), with the monies recovered going to a prescribed charity, currently the Access to Justice Foundation. Previously, section 194 only enabled the "civil courts" (the civil division of the Court of Appeal, the High Court and county courts) to make such orders.

Costs in criminal cases

Section 62 and Schedules 7 and 8: Costs in criminal cases

336.   *Subsection (1)* gives effect to Schedule 7, which amends the Prosecution of Offences Act 1985 ("POA 1985") by limiting the costs, including legal costs (that is, lawyers' fees, charges and disbursements, including expert witness costs) that may be awarded as part of a "defendant's costs order" ("DCO"). Schedule 7 also amends the Criminal Justice Act 1972, the Criminal Justice Act 1988 ("the 1988 Act") and the Extradition Act 2003 by limiting the payment of legal costs in certain proceedings.

---

[15] 2007 c.29

337. *Subsection (2)* gives effect to Schedule 8, which amends the Court Martial Appeals Act 1968 by making changes to the costs that may be awarded to successful appellants and others in the Court Martial Appeal Court and on appeal from that Court.

Schedule 7: Costs in criminal cases

338. Section 16 of the POA 1985 enables courts in England and Wales to order the payment of amounts in respect of costs to be paid out of central funds (that is, out of money provided by Parliament) in certain circumstances. Section 16(6) provides that the amount awarded is to be an amount reasonably sufficient to compensate the person concerned for costs properly incurred. *Paragraph 2* of Schedule 7 inserts new subsections (6A) to (6D) into section 16 of the POA 1985. New subsection (6A) provides that, where the court considers it appropriate, it may reduce the amount awarded to the accused; for example, the court may do so because the accused has been convicted of some offences but acquitted of others. New subsections (6C) and (6D) clarify the existing procedure by which the court makes a costs order in favour of an acquitted defendant or successful appellant. New subsection (6B) provides that orders made by the court under subsections (6) and (6A) have effect subject to new section 16A and regulations made by the Lord Chancellor under new section 20(1A)(d). The effect of section 16A is to limit the circumstances in which a defendant's costs order can include amounts in respect of legal costs. Regulations under section 20(1A)(d) may have the effect that the amount awarded is an amount that is less than an amount which the court considers is reasonably sufficient to compensate the person for the costs incurred.

339. *Paragraph 3* of Schedule 7 inserts a new section 16A in the POA 1985. New section 16A(1) provides that a DCO may not include an amount in respect of legal costs, subject to the following provisions of that section. Section 16A(2) and (3) provide that such an amount can be awarded if the accused is an individual, as opposed to a company or other body, and the order is made (a) in the magistrates' court, (b) on appeal to the Crown Court against a magistrates' court conviction or sentence, or (c) in the Court of Appeal in limited circumstances relating to a defendant who has been found not guilty by reason of insanity, or has been found unfit to stand trial, or having been found unfit to stand trial, has been found to have done the act or made the omission alleged against him.

340. New section 16A(4) provides that a DCO made by the High Court or Court of Appeal can include an amount in respect of legal costs in relation to the costs of an individual defendant in proceedings in the court below, where those proceedings were either in a magistrates' court or were proceedings on appeal to the Crown Court against a magistrates' court conviction or sentence (as those courts would have been able to award legal costs in those proceedings).

341. Section 16A(5) provides that a DCO can include an amount in respect of legal costs incurred in proceedings in the Supreme Court.

342. Section 16A(6) provides that the Lord Chancellor may make regulations that alter the availability of legal costs by adding, modifying or removing an exception to the availability of legal costs. The Lord Chancellor's regulations may provide for an

exception to arise where a determination has been made by a person specified in the regulations. This would allow the Lord Chancellor to prescribe that legal costs are not to be available in respect of cases that do not pass the interests of justice test.

343. Section 16A(7) provides that regulations under *subsection (6)* may not remove or limit the Supreme Court's power to award legal costs incurred in proceedings before it.

344. New section 16A(8) provides that where a court makes a DCO that includes legal costs, the order must contain a statement to this effect.

345. New section 16A(9) provides that amounts awarded by a court in respect of legal costs, other than legal costs incurred in proceedings before the Supreme Court, may not exceed an amount specified in regulations by the Lord Chancellor.

346. New section 16A(10) explains what is meant by "legal costs".

347. *Paragraph 4* of Schedule 7 inserts new subsections (2A), (2B) and (2C) into section 17 of the POA 1985. These subsections are the same as new subsections (6A), (6C) and (6D) of section 16 discussed in paragraph 337 above and apply in respect of private prosecutors. They clarify the procedure to be followed where a court considers that a private prosecutor should recover a sum in respect of his or her costs.

348. *Paragraph 5* of Schedule 7 inserts a new subsection (3ZA) into section 19 of the POA 1985. Section 19(3) provides that the Lord Chancellor may make regulations in respect of the costs of witnesses, and other persons attending court, such as an interpreter, or a person appointed to put the case for the defence where the defendant is unfit to be tried, or is prevented from cross-examining a witness in person. New subsection (3ZA) provides that the requirement that regulations made under section 19(3) make provision for the payment of an amount that the court considers reasonably necessary to compensate the person concerned is subject to regulations under section 20(1A)(d).

349. *Paragraph 5* also inserts new subsections (4A), (4B) and (4C) into section 19 of the POA 1985. They provide that an order made in favour of an appellant in the Court of Appeal who is not in custody may not require the payment of an amount in respect of legal costs unless regulations provide otherwise. Any such order is subject to regulations made by the Lord Chancellor under section 20(1A)(d), which may have the effect that the amount awarded is an amount that is less than an amount which the court considers is reasonably sufficient to compensate the person for the costs incurred.

350. *Paragraph 6* of Schedule 7 inserts a new subsection (1A) into section 20 of the POA 1985. New subsection (1A) provides that the Lord Chancellor may make regulations in respect of amounts that may be paid in pursuance of a costs order. Subsection 20(1A)(a) provides that such regulations can specify rates or scales or make other provision as to the calculation of the amounts to be paid. It is intended that regulations will provide for the payment of amounts in respect of legal costs that are broadly equivalent to legal aid rates.

351. New subsection (1A)(b) provides that regulations may make provision as to the circumstances in which amounts can be paid or ordered to be paid. New subsection (1A)(c) provides that regulations may provide that the amounts required to be paid by a costs order are to be calculated having regard to regulations under paragraphs (a) and (b). This is intended to enable courts to summarily assess the amount to be awarded, using the amounts set out in the regulations as guidance. New subsection (1A)(d) provides that regulations may require the amount of such orders to be fixed in accordance with such regulations. This is likely to be relevant when the court, instead of summarily assessing the amount of the order, directs that the sum be assessed by a determining officer. The amount that results from the application of the regulations does not need to be reasonably sufficient or necessary to compensate the recipient, except in respect of costs incurred in proceedings in the Supreme Court and in the case of costs orders made under section 17 of the POA 1985. New subsection (1A)(e) provides for the regulations to make provision providing for the review of determinations of amounts required to be paid.

352. *Paragraph 8* of Schedule 7 amends section 29 of the POA 1985 to make the powers to make regulations under sections 16A(6) and 19(4B) subject to the affirmative resolution procedure. Those powers can be used to alter the circumstances in which amounts in respect of legal costs may be awarded by a court.

353. *Paragraph 9* of Schedule 7 amends section 36 of the Criminal Justice Act 1972, which relates to references by the Attorney General on a point of law following acquittal on indictment. It provides that the court's power to order the payment of costs out of central funds is subject to regulations made under section 20(1A)(d) of the POA 1985 (which is applied for the purposes of this section). It also provides that orders may not be made for the payment out of central funds of amounts in respect of legal costs incurred in proceedings on the reference in the Court of Appeal. Section 14(f) of this Act provides that proceedings on a point of law following acquittal on indictment are "criminal proceedings" for the purposes of legal aid.

354. *Paragraph 11* of Schedule 7 amends Schedule 3 to the 1988 Act, which relates to references by the Attorney General to the Court of Appeal or Supreme Court in relation to a sentence of the Crown Court that appears to be unduly lenient. It provides that, in England and Wales, the court's power to order the payment of costs out of central funds is subject to regulations made under section 20(1A)(d) of the POA 1985 (which is applied for the purposes of this section). It also provides that orders may not be made for the payment out of central funds of amounts in respect of legal costs incurred in proceedings in the Court of Appeal. Section 14(b) of the Legal Aid, Sentencing and Punishment of Offenders Act 2012 provides that proceedings for dealing with an individual convicted of an offence, which includes references under the 1988 Act, are "criminal proceedings" for the purposes of legal aid. Paragraph 11 also contains consequential provisions to preserve the existing arrangements in relation to costs for Northern Ireland.

355. *Paragraph 13* amends section 61 of the Extradition Act 2003 (costs where discharge ordered) by inserting new subsections (5A) and (5B). New subsection (5A) provides that, in England and Wales, an order for costs is to be made in accordance with new sections 62A and 62B. New subsection (5B) provides that an order for costs in

Scotland and Northern Ireland under subsection (5) is to be determined in accordance with subsections (6) to (9) so that the existing arrangements are preserved for those jurisdictions.

356.   *Paragraph 14* omits subsections (1) and (2) of section 62 of the Extradition Act 2003. Subsection (1) and (2) provide that, in respect of England and Wales, subsections (1) and (3) of section 20 of the POA 1985 apply in relation to section 61 of the Extradition Act 2003 as they apply to Part 2 of the POA 1985.

357.   *Paragraph 15* inserts new sections 62A and 62B into the Extradition Act 2003. New section 62A(1) to (5) makes provision equivalent to sections 16(6) to 16(6D) of the POA 1985 (i.e. provision as to the amount to be awarded pursuant to an order for costs and the calculation of that amount). New subsection (6) of section 62A provides that section 20(1A) to (1C) and (3) of the POA 1985 (regulations as to amounts ordered to be paid out of central funds) apply for the purposes of orders under section 61 as they apply for the purposes of orders under section 16 of the POA 1985. New section 62B provides that, in England and Wales, an order under section 61(5) may not include an amount in respect of legal costs unless those legal costs were incurred in the magistrates' court or the Supreme Court. The Lord Chancellor may, by regulations, make provision about exceptions from the prohibition against the award of legal costs, but such regulations cannot affect the Supreme Court's power to award an amount in respect of legal costs incurred in proceedings before it.

358.   *Paragraph 16* makes amendments of section 134 of the Extradition Act 2003 (costs where discharge ordered) equivalent to the amendments of section 61 of that Act.

359.   *Paragraphs 20 to 22* provide that the amendments to the POA 1985, the Criminal Justice Act 1972, the 1988 Act and the Extradition Act 2003 do not affect a person's entitlement to costs in respect of proceedings and references commenced prior to commencement of the relevant provisions.

Schedule 8: Costs in criminal cases: service courts
360.   Schedule 8 makes similar provision in relation to the legal costs of an appellant in the Court Martial Appeal Court as the provision made in relation to civilian courts in Schedule 7. It also removes the restriction on successful appellants against sentence receiving costs (see *paragraph 2(2))*.

Part 3: Sentencing and punishment of offenders

Chapter 1: Sentencing
General
Section 63: Duty to consider compensation order
361.   Section 63 amends section 130 of the Powers of Criminal Courts (Sentencing) Act 2000 and strengthens the obligation on the court to consider ordering a person convicted of an offence to pay compensation.

362.   The section inserts a new subsection (2A) in section 130, which places the court under an express duty to consider making a compensation order in any case where it is empowered to do so under that section. Compensation may be ordered for any loss or damage, personal injury or bereavement, or to make payments for funeral.

363.   *Subsection (2)* inserts a similar provision into the Armed Forces Act 2006.

Section 64: Duty to give reasons for and to explain effect of sentence

364.   Section 64 replaces the existing section 174 of the 2003 Act with a new version of that section retaining a general duty to explain a sentence and reducing the specific requirements on the court.

365.   The substituted version of section 174 retains, in *subsection (2)*, the general duty on a court to explain in open court and in ordinary language the court's reasons for deciding on a sentence. The substituted section 174 also retains the general duty, in *subsection (3)*, to explain to an offender the effect of the sentence and the implications of the offender not complying with the sentence.

366.   *Subsection (4)* makes corresponding amendments to the Armed Forces Act 2006.

367.   The substituted section 174 provides, in *subsection (4)*, that the Criminal Procedure Rules may prescribe cases in which either the duty to state the court's reasons for deciding on the sentence, or the duty to explain the matters mentioned in *subsection (3)* does not apply. It also provides that Criminal Procedure Rules may make provision about how an explanation of the matters mentioned in section *subsection (3)* is to be given.

368.   The substituted section 174 goes on to set out, in *subsections (6) to (8)*, a revised and reduced list of the particular duties on courts to explain aspects of a sentence. These duties include, in *subsection (6)*, identifying relevant sentencing guidelines and explaining how they were applied or why they were not applied. In *subsection (7)* there is a duty to explain the impact on the sentence of a reduction for a guilty plea. In *subsection (8)* a court must explain, in giving a juvenile a discretionary custodial sentence, why a non-custodial sentence could not be justified, and in making a youth rehabilitation order with intensive supervision and surveillance or with fostering, why the order is appropriate.

369.   The substituted section 174 removes specific duties to explain the court's consideration of the thresholds for imposing a custodial sentence or community order. The new section 174 also removes the particular exception from the general duty to explain a sentence where the sentence is fixed by law (mandatory minimum sentences). These considerations are now covered by the general duty on courts contained in *subsections (2) and (3)* of the substituted section 174.

370.   Section 65: Sentencing where there is aggravation related to transgender identity

371.   Section 65 amends section 146 of the 2003 Act. Section 146 provides that it is a factor increasing the seriousness of an offence, which affects the severity of the sentence, if the offender demonstrates, or was motivated by, hostility based on the

victim's sexual orientation or disability. The section adds transgender identity (or presumed transgender identity) to the personal characteristics which will constitute an aggravating factor. The umbrella term "transgender" is not defined but *subsection (6)* (which inserts new subsection (6) into section 146) makes it clear that "being transgender" includes, but is not limited to, being transsexual.

372.   Section 65 also amends Schedule 21 to the 2003 Act, which sets out the starting points which a court should adopt when determining a minimum term for a mandatory life sentence imposed for murder.

Community orders
Section 66: Duration of community order
373.   Section 66 makes provision about when a community order comes to an end.

374.   Currently a community order must specify a date by which all the requirements in the order must have been complied with. This date may not be more than three years after the date of the order. However, there is no express provision about when the order itself comes to an end.

375.   *Subsections (1) and (2)* amend section 177(5) of the 2003 Act and insert new subsections (5A) and (5B). These amendments provide that a community order comes to an end on the date specified under section 177(5). (This is subject to specific provision in relation to an unpaid work requirement, where the order continues in force until the requirement is complied with.) Where an order imposes two or more requirements, a court may specify end dates for each of those requirements, and where it does so, the last of those end dates must be the same as the date specified under section 177(5) (that is, the date at which the order comes to an end).

376.   *Subsections (3) and (4)* allow magistrates' courts and the Crown Court respectively to extend the duration of an order by up to 6 months where the offender has breached a requirement in an order.

377.   *Subsection (5)* allows magistrates' courts and the Crown Court to extend the duration of an order otherwise than for breach of the order.

Section 67: Breach of community order
378.   Section 67 amends Schedule 8 to the 2003 Act, which makes provision about breach of a requirement imposed as part of a community order and a court's powers in relation to such a breach.

379.   Schedule 8 already provides a court with the option of dealing with breach of an order by either varying the order to make its requirements more onerous (for example, by extending the duration of a requirement or adding a new one), or revoking the order and re-sentencing the offender as if the offender had just been convicted. There is currently no option to take no action.

380.   Schedule 8 provides that in dealing with an offender for breach the court must take into account the extent to which he has already complied with the order. If the

offender has willfully and persistently failed to comply with a community order the court can re-sentence the offender to custody even if the original offence was not serious enough to justify a custodial sentence.

381.   The section gives a court the option of taking no action in relation to a breach. It also gives a court a new power to fine an offender in relation to a breach (and in that case the order will continue in force).

382.   *Subsection (2)* amends paragraph 9(1) of Schedule 8 in two ways: it provides a magistrates' court with the option of taking no action; and it provides the court with a new power to impose a fine on the offender of not more than £2,500 in relation to the breach.

383.   *Subsection (5)* makes substantially the same provision as *subsection (2)*, but in relation to the Crown Court

384.   *Subsection (7)* inserts a new provision giving the Secretary of State a power by order (subject to the negative Parliamentary procedure) to amend the maximum amount of a fine which may be imposed by the magistrates' court or Crown Court in relation to a breach of a community order. The power may only be exercised if it appears to the Secretary of State that there has been a change in the value of money. The power replicates the power of the courts in relation to breach of a youth rehabilitation order (see paragraph 10 of Schedule 2 to the 2008 Act).

Suspended sentence orders
Section 68 and Schedule 9: Changes to powers to make suspended sentence order
385.   Section 68 amends provisions relating to suspended sentences. Currently a court cannot suspend prison sentences that are longer than 12 months. The courts are also currently required to attach at least one "community requirement" to a suspended sentence even if they consider that no community requirement is necessary in the circumstances. (Community requirements are available to address issues of offender behaviour through treatment programmes such as alcohol or drug addiction and poor cognitive skills.)

386.   *Subsection (1)* amends section 189 of the 2003 Act to enable courts to suspend longer sentences of imprisonment, namely those between 14 days and two years. The amended section also provides the court with discretion as to whether or not to impose community requirements. The section retains the current position whereby the sentence of imprisonment will not take effect unless the offender fails to comply with a community requirement or is convicted of a further offence during the period of suspension.

387.   *Subsection (2)* provides that, where a court imposes consecutive sentences, the power to make a suspended sentence order is limited to cases where the sentence does not exceed two years in total.

388.   *Subsections (3) and (4)* clarify that the provisions relating to the length of supervision periods (the period during which the offender is subject to one or more community requirements) apply only to those orders with community requirements.

389.　*Subsection (6)* gives effect to Schedule 9, which makes consequential and transitional provision (see below).

390.　*Subsection (7)* provides that the new provisions apply to offences committed before, and after, the section comes into force where the offender is sentenced after the section comes into force.

Schedule 9: Changes to powers to make suspended sentence orders: consequential and transitory provision

391.　*Paragraphs 1 to 19* of Schedule 9 make various amendments which are consequential on the changes to powers to make suspended sentence orders introduced by section 68, in particular to ensure requirements that are only appropriate for suspended sentences with community requirements do not apply where they would be inappropriate or unnecessary for suspended sentence without community requirements.

392.　*Paragraph 20* of Schedule 9 contains a transitory provision to apply the new provisions to detention in young offender institutions, since pending the coming into force of section 61 of the Criminal Justice and Court Services Act 2000 (which will abolish a sentence of detention in a young offender institution), such a sentence is still possible.

Section 69: Fine for breach of suspended sentence order

393.　At present the court has no power to impose a fine for breach of a suspended sentence order. Section 69 inserts a new provision into paragraph 8 of Schedule 12 to the 2003 Act. This will enable the court to impose a fine of up to £2,500 for breach of a suspended sentence order where it decides not to give effect to the custodial sentence.

394.　A suspended sentence order is breached where an offender fails to comply with any community requirement or is convicted of another offence during the period for which the sentence is suspended. Any fine is enforced as it would be had it been imposed on conviction

395.　*Subsection (3)* inserts a new provision giving the Secretary of State a power by order (subject to the negative Parliamentary procedure) to amend the maximum amount of a fine which may be imposed by the magistrates' court or Crown Court in relation to a breach of a suspended sentence order. The power may only be exercised if it appears to the Secretary of State that there has been a change in the value of money. The power replicates the power of the courts in relation to breach of a youth rehabilitation order (see paragraph 10 of Schedule 2 to the 2008 Act). It also replicates a power conferred by section 67(7) of the Act in relation to a fine for breach of a community order.

Requirements under community orders and suspended sentence orders
Section 70: Programme requirement

396.　Section 70 amends section 202 of the 2003 Act which makes provision in relation to "programme requirements". These may be imposed as part of a community order or a suspended sentence order with a view to addressing particular aspects of offender behaviour such as treatment of alcohol or drug addiction and poor cognitive skills.

397.   *Subsection (4)* amends section 202(1) of the 2003 Act by reducing the number of matters the court must specify when imposing a programme requirement. It removes the requirement for a court to specify (a) the particular accredited programme in which the offender must participate, and (b) the place at which the offender must participate in an accredited programme. It retains the requirement for a court to specify the number of days on which the offender must take part in an accredited programme. By the amendments to section 202(6) of the 2003 Act, it will be for the responsible officer to determine those matters.

398.   *Subsection (5)* repeals section 202(4) and (5) of the 2003 Act, which specify a number of conditions that have to be met before a court may impose a programme requirement. These conditions currently require a court to include only certain accredited programmes, and prevent the court from including a programme requirement if compliance with that requirement would involve the co-operation of someone other than the offender and the responsible officer, unless that person has consented. The effect of *subsection (5)* is that those conditions will no longer apply.

Section 71: Curfew requirement

399.   Section 71 amends section 204 of the 2003 Act, which makes provision in relation to curfew requirements.

400.   *Subsection (2)* amends section 204(2) by increasing the maximum period in any day for which the court may impose a curfew requirement from twelve to sixteen hours.

401.   *Subsection (3)* amends section 204(3) by increasing the maximum period for which a curfew requirement may be imposed from six to twelve months from the date on which the community order is made.

402.   It remains the case that, before imposing a curfew requirement, the court must obtain and consider the effect that the curfew might have on other people living at the curfew address. Compliance with a curfew requirement is normally monitored electronically by the offender wearing a 'tag'.

Section 72: Foreign travel prohibition requirement

403.   Section 72 amends sections 177 and 190 of the 2003 Act to enable a court to impose a prohibition on foreign travel as a requirement in a community order or suspended sentence order. The effect of the new requirement is to prohibit travel to a country or countries (or territory or territories) outside the British Islands (the United Kingdom, the Channel Islands and the Isle of Man).

404.   Currently courts can already impose a number of requirements that restrict offenders' movements in some way. These include curfews, residence requirements, and exclusion requirements. However, there is no requirement which gives courts an express power to prohibit an offender from travelling outside the British Islands.

Section 73: Mental health treatment requirement

405.   Section 73 amends section 207 of the 2003 Act which makes provision about mental health treatment requirements in community orders or suspended sentence orders.

406.   Currently, a court cannot make a mental health treatment requirement unless it is satisfied on the evidence of a registered medical practitioner approved for the purposes of section 12 of the Mental Health Act 1983 that the mental condition of the offender requires treatment and may be susceptible to it, and other disposals under the Mental Health Act 1983 are not warranted.

407.   Section 73 removes the condition that a court can only impose a mental health treatment requirement on the evidence of a registered mental health practitioner approved for the purposes of section 12. It remains the case that the court may not include a mental health treatment requirement unless the offender has expressed willingness to comply with it.

Section 74: Drug rehabilitation requirement

408.   Section 74 amends section 209 of the 2003 Act, which makes provision in relation to drug rehabilitation requirements.

409.   It removes the requirement that the treatment and testing period of a drug rehabilitation requirement must be at least six months. The effect of this is that there will be no minimum treatment and testing period. The change provides the court with greater discretion in determining the appropriate length of the requirement.

Section 75: Alcohol treatment requirement

410.   Section 75 amends section 212 of the 2003 Act, which makes provision in relation to alcohol treatment requirements.

411.   It removes the requirement that the period of an alcohol treatment requirement must be at least six months. The effect of this is that there will be no minimum period. The change provides the court with greater discretion in determining the appropriate length of the requirement.

Section 76: Alcohol abstinence and monitoring requirement

412.   Section 76 inserts new section 212A into the 2003 Act. This has the effect of creating a new alcohol abstinence and monitoring requirement which may be imposed as a requirement of a community order or suspended sentence order.

413.   Under new section 212A(1)(a) a court has the power to order an offender either to abstain from consuming alcohol for a specified period or not to consume alcohol so that during a specified period they have a level of alcohol higher than a level specified by the order in their body. An offender on whom such a requirement is imposed would have to submit to monitoring for the purposes of ascertaining whether they were complying with the requirement under new section 212A(1)(a).

414.   New section 212A(2) limits the maximum period of the new requirement to 120 days. (However, *subsection (7)* of section 76 amends section 223(3) of the 2003 Act with the effect that the Secretary of State has a power to amend the maximum period. This power would be exercisable subject to the affirmative resolution procedure, and is common to a number of other requirements.)

415. New section 212A(3) gives the Secretary of State a power to prescribe a minimum period for the requirement.

416. New section 212A(4) gives the Secretary of State a power to prescribe the level of alcohol an offender must not exceed under a requirement set out under new section 212A(1)(a)(ii). Such a requirement may not be imposed unless an order has been made to prescribe alcohol levels. An order which prescribes alcohol levels may do so by reference to the proportion of alcohol in the offender's breath, blood, urine or sweat, or by some other means.

417. New section 212A(6) gives the Secretary of State a power by order to prescribe arrangements for monitoring of compliance with the requirement. Such an order may prescribe arrangements for monitoring by electronic or other means.

418. New section 212A(8) to (12) makes provision about the conditions for imposing the new requirement. There are four conditions.

419. The first is that consumption of alcohol must be an element of the offence before the court, or the court must be satisfied that consumption of alcohol was a contributing factor to the commission of the offence.

420. The second is that the court must be satisfied that the offender is not dependent on alcohol.

421. The third is that the court must not include an alcohol treatment requirement (under section 212 of the 2003 Act) in the order.

422. The fourth is that the court must have been notified by the Secretary of State that arrangements for monitoring have been made in the local justice area.

423. *Subsections (2) to (11)* of section 76 make further amendments to the 2003 Act and the Armed Forces Act 2006 as a consequence of the creation of the new requirement. *Subsection (6)* amends section 215 of the 2003 Act to prevent the court from imposing an electronic monitoring requirement in respect of the new requirement. This is because electronic monitoring provisions may be included in the new requirement itself (see new section 212A(7)(a)).

Section 77: Piloting of alcohol abstinence and monitoring requirements
424. Section 77 requires the provisions creating the new alcohol abstinence and monitoring requirement to be commenced initially for the purposes of a pilot. *Subsection (1)* allows the Secretary of State (after having made a piloting order or orders) to make a general commencement order. Under *subsection (5)(a)* an order made by the Secretary of State may amend the alcohol abstinence and monitoring requirement provisions under section 76 to enable the provisions to be brought into force generally with amendments, and *subsection (5)(b)* would allow the Secretary of State to amend other provisions of the Act in consequence of these changes. *Subsection (6)(a)* makes it clear that *subsection (5)(a)* includes a power to confer order or rule making powers on the Secretary of State.

425.   *Subsection (7)* contains a power exercisable by the Secretary of State, after having made a piloting order or orders, to make an order to repeal section 76, to amend the 2003 Act to reverse the effect of that section on that Act or to make other consequential amendments or repeals.

426.   *Subsection (9)* provides for an order under the new section to be made by statutory instrument. *Subsection (10)* provides that a general commencement order, or an order to amend or to repeal section 76, may not be made unless the order has been laid before and approved by each House of Parliament.

Section 78: Overseas community orders and service community orders

427.   Section 78 makes amendments to provisions of the Armed Forces Act 2006 relating to both service and overseas community orders which can be made by service courts. These amendments flow from changes made to the 2003 Act by Chapter 1 of Part 3 of the Act.

428.   *Subsections (2) and (3)* provide that the foreign travel prohibition requirement introduced by section 67 of the Act and the alcohol abstinence and monitoring requirement introduced by section 76 are not available for inclusion as a requirement in an overseas community order.

429.   *Subsection (4)* makes provision which applies in the Services context the Act provisions about the duration of community orders made by civilian courts. *Subsections (6) and (8)* make a change to the provisions about overseas and service community orders that is consequential on section 66(5).

430.   *Subsections (5) and (9)* make provision in relation to the imposition of fines for breaches of overseas community orders.

431.   *Subsection (10)* makes provision which makes a change in the service context which results from the provisions in section 74 to disapply the minimum term of a drug rehabilitation requirement.

432.   As with other amendments made to armed forces legislation, this section is designed to ensure that sentencing law and practice of service courts is, where practicable, aligned with the law and practice of civilian courts in England and Wales.

Youth sentences
Section 79: Referral orders for young offenders

433.   Section 79 amends sections 16 and 17 of the Powers of Criminal Courts (Sentencing) Act 2000 (PCC(S)A 2000), which set out the circumstances in which the court has the power to give a referral order to an offender under the age of 18.

434.   A referral order refers the offender to a youth offender panel and requires the offender to attend meetings of the panel and enter into a contract with the panel to undertake rehabilitative activities for a period of between 3 and 12 months.

435.   Sections 16(2) and 17(1) of the PCC(S)A 2000 impose a duty on a youth court or magistrates' court either to make a referral order or to discharge offenders absolutely where they have pleaded guilty to their first offence (or where they are before the court for more than one offence, at least one of these offences) unless certain exceptions apply. Those exceptions are: if the offence (or at least one of the offences) that the offender is being sentenced for is fixed by law (section 16(1)(a)) or the court proposes to impose a custodial sentence or a hospital order in respect of the offence (or where the offender is before the court for more than one offence, at least one of these offences). Where the exceptions apply the duty does not apply.

436.   Typically, these exceptions apply only in a very few cases so the powers of the court when sentencing a first time offender who has pleaded guilty are very limited. The court can never impose a community sentence on an offender where section 16 of the PCC(S)A 2000 applies.

437.   Sections 16(3) and 17(2) to (2C) of the PCC(S)A 2000 provide a discretionary power for a youth or magistrates' court either to make a referral order or absolutely discharge offenders where they have pleaded guilty to the offence (or where they are before the court for more than one offence, at least one of these offences), even if it is not their first offence. But the court may only do so in circumstances where the offender has not previously received a referral order (section 17(2B)) or has received a referral order on one occasion but is recommended as suitable for another by an 'appropriate officer' (usually an officer of the local youth offending team) (section 17(2C)).

438.   *Subsection (1)* amends section 16(1)(c) of the PCC(S)A 2000 to widen the powers of a youth or magistrates' court to deal with offenders where they have pleaded guilty to their first offence (or where they are before the court for more than one offence, at least one of these offences). As a result of this amendment, where the exceptions in 16(1)(a) and (b) do not apply, the court will no longer have to choose between making a referral order or absolutely discharging the offender: it will now be able to choose to conditionally discharge the offender instead.

439.   *Subsection (2)* amends section 17 PCC(S)A 2000. It removes the existing conditions set out in section 17(2A) to (2C) and amends section 17(2) in order to widen the powers of a youth or magistrates' court to deal with an offender who has pleaded guilty to an offence (or, where the offender is before the court for more than one offence, to at least one of those offences), even if it is not the offender's first offence. As a result of the amendment, the court is no longer prevented from offering referral orders to offenders who have previously received referral orders in the past. There is no limit to the number of referral orders that a repeat offender can receive. The offender does not need to be recommended as suitable for a second or subsequent referral order by an appropriate officer.

Section 80: Breach of detention and training order

440. A detention and training order (DTO) is a custodial sentence for young offenders aged between 12 and 17 created by sections 100 to 107 PCC(S)A 2000. In broad terms, the offender spends the first half of the specified period in custody (detention and training) and the second half in the community subject to various requirements and under the supervision of the youth offending team.

441. *Subsections (2) to (7)* amend section 104 of the PCC(S)A 2000 to extend the powers of the court to punish an offender who has breached their DTO by failing to comply with the supervision requirements imposed on them

442. *Subsection (2)* retains the power of the court to impose a period of detention in punishment for the breach. It also creates a new power for the court to impose an additional period of supervision.

443. *Subsection (3)* inserts new subsections (3A) to (3D), which make further provision about the periods of supervision or detention, into section 104:

- new subsection (3A) sets the maximum period for which the court may impose supervision or detention as a punishment for breach. This is to be the shorter of 3 months or the period beginning with the date of the failure to comply with the requirement and the last day of the term of the DTO.

- new subsection (3B) stipulates how that period is to be determined if the failure to comply with a requirement took place over two or more days.

- new subsection (3C) is especially important as it provides that the court may impose a period of supervision or detention for breach even after the term of the DTO has finished. This means that those subject to a DTO will not be able to avoid being given a further period of detention or supervision by delaying their breach hearings until after the term of their DTO expires as has happened following the case of *H v Doncaster Youth Court, Doncaster Youth Offending Service*[16] where the court had held that a further period of detention could only be imposed from the date on which the court made a finding that the offender had failed to comply with supervision requirements, rather than from the actual failure to comply, and only up to the end of the original DTO period.

- new subsection (3D) provides that where the court imposes a period of detention or supervision for breach, it takes immediate effect and can overlap with a period of supervision under the DTO.

444. *Subsection (4)* inserts new section 104(4A) into the PCC(S)A 2000. This provides that where an offender is over 18 when a court orders a further period of detention in respect of a breach of a DTO, the offender will be sent to prison. This subsection needs to be read with section 74(8) of the Act which provides that an offender aged between 18 and 21 will not be sent to prison under section 104(4A) until such time as

---

[16] [2008] EWHC 3463

section 61 of the Criminal Justice and Court Services Act 2000 is commenced (and the sentence of detention in a young offenders institution is abolished). Until that time 18 to 21 year olds will be sent to youth detention accommodation, which includes young offender institutions (see section 107 of the PCC(S)A 2000).

445. *Subsection (6)* extends the right of appeal to the Crown Court that currently exists where an offender is given a further period of detention for breach of a DTO to the new power to impose an additional period of supervision.

446. *Subsection (7)* inserts new sections 104A and 104B into the PCC(S)A 2000. New section 104A applies certain provision in the PCC(S)A 2000 relating to DTOs to orders under section 104(3)(aa) that an offender serve a further period of supervision, with the necessary modifications:

- section 104A(1) and (2) applies section 103 (which provides for how a period of supervision under a DTO operates);

- section 104A(3) to (5) applies section 104 (which deals with breach of DTO supervision requirements) and section 105 (which makes provision for when an offender commits an offence when subject to supervision).

447. In broad terms, the further period of supervision works in a similar way to the period of supervision under a DTO. In particular, requirements can be imposed on the offender under section 103 of the PCC(S)A 2000, as applied, and enforced under section 104 of that Act, again as applied. And, if the offender commits an imprisonable offence while subject to a further period of supervision, then the offender can be detained in youth detention accommodation under section 105, as applied.

448. The fact that a court can deal with an offender who breaches requirements imposed in respect of a further period of supervision in the same way that it can deal with someone who has breached the supervision requirements of a DTO, means that there could be a series of orders under section 104(3)(aa). If an offender breaches a DTO and is given a further of supervision which the offender then also breaches, the court can once again respond by imposing further supervision (or detention or a fine). And if requirements attached to that further period of supervision are also then breached, another period of supervision could be ordered in respect of that breach and so on. This continues to be the case until the offender completes the order of the court without breaching it.

449. New section 104B provides for the interaction between the new power to impose periods of detention beyond the end of the original DTO and other sentences. Subsections (1) to (4) provide for the interaction between a period of further detention and a DTO. New subsection 104B(5) provides a power for the Secretary of State to make regulations to provide for the interaction between a period of detention imposed for breach and custodial sentences other than a DTO.

450.   A further period of detention can be imposed for breach after the term of the DTO has ended. It can also be imposed in respect of the breach of a requirement attached to a period of further supervision under section 104(3)(aa), which may itself have been imposed after the end of the DTO. It is therefore possible for a period of detention to be imposed under section 104(3)(a) after the offender has turned 18 or even 21. For this reason it is necessary to set out for the courts how the breach period will interact with adult sentences.

451.   *Subsections (10) and (11)* apply the provision made by the section to any breach of a DTO that occurs after commencement.

Section 81: Youth rehabilitation order: curfew requirement

452.   A youth rehabilitation order is a community sentence provided for by the 2008 Act. As part of the sentence a court may impose one or more of 18 different requirements that the offender must comply with for a period of up to three years. The requirements can include curfew, supervision and mental health treatment requirements. These requirements are similar to requirements that can be attached to community orders for adults.

453.   Section 81 mirrors the amendments to the curfew requirement for community orders in section 71 of the Act by increasing the maximum number of hours in a day for which a curfew can be imposed from twelve to sixteen hours a day and the length of time for which a curfew requirement may be imposed from six to twelve months.

Section 82: Youth rehabilitation order: mental health treatment requirement

454.   Section 82 amends paragraph 20 of Schedule 1 to the 2008 Act to make provision for mental health treatment requirements in youth rehabilitation orders. It mirrors the amendments to mental health treatment requirements in section 73 for adults by removing the requirement for evidence from a medical practitioner approved for the purposes of section 12 of the Mental Health Act 1983. It remains the case that the court cannot include a mental treatment requirement unless the youth has expressed a willingness to comply with it.

Section 83: Youth rehabilitation order: duration

455.   This section amends the current provisions in Schedules 1 and 2 to the the 2008 Act which set out the duration of youth rehabilitation orders. Under the current provisions where an order has multiple requirements which may themselves be time limited it can be unclear when the order is completed. In some cases this can result in the requirements being completed before the end date of the order requiring the case to be returned to court to revoke the order.

456.   *Subsection (1)* amends Schedule 1 to the 2008 Act to enable the court to specify different completion dates for different requirements attached to an order and for the end date of the order to be the same as the last completion date for a requirement.

457.   *Subsection (2)* inserts new sub-paragraphs (6A) to (6D) in paragraph 6 of Schedule 2 to allow a magistrates' court to extend the end date of an order by up to 6 months where a further requirement is imposed but only on one occasion. If the order is

extended under these provisions then it may extend beyond the three year maximum length set out in Schedule 1.

458.   *Subsection (3)* inserts new sub-paragraphs (6A) to (6D) in paragraph 8 of Schedule 2 which makes the same amendments to the powers in the Crown Court as subsection (2) does to the powers of the magistrates' court.

459.   *Subsection (5)* inserts a new paragraph 16A in Schedule 2 relating to the exercise of powers of the magistrates' court or Crown court when dealing with breach of a youth rehabilitation order to cancel or replace requirements in the order. Sub-paragraph (1) of new paragraph 16A allows a court to amend the end date of an order where either the offender or responsible officer requests this. Further provisions limit the extension of the end date to a maximum period of 6 months beyond the end date of the original order and allow the overall length of the order to extend beyond the maximum of three years where the order is so extended. This power to extend is limited to one occasion only. Sub-paragraph (6) provides that the court amending the length of the order must be a youth court where the offender is aged under 18 at the time the application to extend is made or an adult magistrates' court where the offender has reached the age of 18.

Section 84: Youth rehabilitation order: fine for breach

460.   Section 84 provides for the fine available to a court to deal with breach of a youth rehabilitation order under Schedule 2 to the 2008 Act to be increased to a maximum amount of £2,500. Currently the maximum fine in both the magistrates' courts and the Crown Court is £250 if the offender is aged under 14, or £1,000 in any other case.

Fines
Section 85: Removal of limit on certain fines on conviction by magistrates' court

461.   Section 85 removes limits on fines of £5,000 or more (however that amount is expressed) on conviction by the magistrates' court. The section applies to fines set out in primary and secondary legislation. The section also modifies powers to create offences which are punishable on summary conviction by a fine with a limit of £5,000 or more, so that they are punishable by a fine of any amount. The section gives the Secretary of State a power to disapply the removal of limits and to set alternative limits, subject to certain restrictions. The section applies to sentences on summary conviction, i.e. on conviction in a magistrates' court for an offence which is triable only summarily or triable either way (see *subsection (16)*).

462.   *Subsection (1)* provides that relevant offences which are punishable on summary conviction by fines of £5,000 or more (however that sum is expressed), are punishable by a fine of any amount. Where the maximum amount of a fine which may be imposed on summary conviction is £5,000, that sum is expressed in different provisions in different ways. In some cases the amount is expressed as the specific figure of £5,000. In some cases it is expressed as 'an amount not exceeding the prescribed sum,' or 'the statutory maximum,' or 'level 5 on the standard scale.' In each case the amount is £5,000. This subsection applies in respect of each of those formulations, and any other formulation which has the same effect.

463.   *Subsection (2)* provides that where a relevant power could be exercised to create an offence punishable on summary conviction by a fine of £5,000 or more, the power may be exercised to create an offence punishable by a fine of any amount.

464.   *Subsection (3)* provides that an offence or power is relevant if it is a common law offence or it is contained in an Act or secondary legislation immediately before *subsection (1)* of this section comes into force. It is a relevant offence or power whether or not it is in force at that time.

465.   *Subsection (4)* sets out a series of limitations on the provisions in *subsections (1) and (2)*. These limitations relate to fines for offences committed before the day on which *subsection (1)* of this section comes into force, to the operation of restrictions on fines that may be imposed on a person under 18, and to fines imposed by a Crown Court following committal for sentence from the magistrates' court, where the Crown Court is exercising its own sentencing jurisdiction.

466.   *Subsection (5)* gives the Secretary of State powers by regulations to disapply *subsection (1) or (2)*. *Subsection (6)* gives the Secretary of State power by regulations to make alternative provision in respect of offences or powers in respect of which the power in *subsection (5)* is exercised.

467.   *Subsections (7) and (8)* deal with the situation where a fine is expressed as a proportion of £5,000 (however expressed). For instance, some offences under the Companies Act 2006 contain offences punishable by a fine of an amount per day not exceeding 10% of the statutory maximum. The Secretary of State may make regulations to specify or describe a higher amount than £5,000 for these purposes

468.   *Subsection (9)* imposes the same limitations in respect of regulations under section 85 as are imposed by *subsection (4)* (described above).

469.   *Subsections (10) and (11)* make further provision about the scope of the powers to make regulations in this section.

470.   *Subsections (12) and (13)* provide that regulations made under this section are to be made by statutory instrument, using the affirmative resolution procedure.

471.   *Subsection (14)* makes particular provision to deal with the possibility that the power under the Criminal Justice Act 1982 to raise the sum specified as level 5 on the standard scale to reflect increases in the value of money may be exercised before the day on which *subsection (1)* of this section comes into force. It provides that, if that happens, references in this section to £5,000 have effect as if they were references to the new sum.

Section 86: Power to increase certain other fines on conviction by magistrates' court

472.   Section 86 makes provision in relation to fines or maximum fines of fixed amounts which are less than £5,000. (Such fines are not affected by section 85(1) or (2). Nor are they affected by the powers in section 88, which only relate to amounts expressed as levels 1 to 4 on the standard scale.)

473.   *Subsections (1) and (2)* provide that the Secretary of State may make regulations in respect of relevant offences which are punishable by a fine of a fixed amount (i.e. a sum set out as a figure in the legislation) of less than £5,000. The regulations may specify or describe an amount in place of the original amount.

474.   *Subsections (3) and (4)* provide that the Secretary of State may make regulations in respect of powers to create offences which are punishable by a fine of a fixed amount (i.e. a sum set out as a figure in the legislation) of less than £5,000. The regulations may specify or describe an amount in place of the original amount.

475.   *Subsection (5)* provides that the amount which may be specified or described may not exceed the greater of £5,000 or the sum specified as level 4 on the standard scale. (Section 88 gives the Secretary of State powers to amend levels 1 to 4 on the standard scale.)

476.   *Subsection (6)* sets out a series of limitations on the powers in this section. These limitations relate to fines for offences committed before the day on which section 85(1) comes into force, to the operation of restrictions on fines that may be imposed on a person under 18, and to fines imposed by a Crown Court following committal for sentence from the magistrates' court, where the Crown Court is exercising its own sentencing jurisdiction.

477.   *Subsections (7) and (8)* make further provision about the scope of the powers to make regulations in this section.

478.   *Subsections (9) and (10)* provide that regulations made under this section are to be made by statutory instrument, using the affirmative resolution procedure.

479.   *Subsection (11)* makes particular provision to deal with the possibility that the power under the Criminal Justice Act 1982 to raise the sum specified as level 5 on the standard scale to reflect increases in the value of money may be exercised before the day on which section 86(1) comes into force. It provides that, if that happens, references in this section to £5,000 have effect as if they were references to the new sum.

Section 87: Power to amend standard scale of fines for summary offences
480.   Section 87 gives the Secretary of State power by order to alter the sums specified as levels 1 to 4 on the standard scale of fines for summary offences.

481.   *Subsection (1)* provides that the Secretary of State may by order substitute for the sums specified as levels 1 to 4 on the standard scale, such sums as the Secretary of State considers appropriate. Level 1 is currently £200, level 2 is £500, level 3 is £1,000 and level 4 is £2,500.

482.   *Subsection (2)* prevents the Secretary of State from altering the sums in a way which alters the ratio of the levels to each other.

483.   *Subsections (5) and (6)* provide that orders made under this section are to be made by statutory instrument, using the affirmative resolution procedure.

484.   *Subsection (7)* provides that an order altering the sums does not affect fines for offences committed before the order comes into force.

Section 88: Withdrawal of warrants of control issued by fines officer

485.   Section 88 relates to the withdrawal of "warrants of control", as the current warrants of distress will be termed when the provisions in Part 3 of the Tribunals, Courts and Enforcement Act 2007 come into force (until then, they will continue, by way of transitional saving, to be termed warrants of distress). Section 88 makes a number of amendments to Schedule 5 of the Courts Act 2003 including the insertion of four new paragraphs.

486.   Section 88(4) inserts a new paragraph 37A into Schedule 5 to the Courts Act 2003. Paragraph 37A allows a fines officer, in certain circumstances, to issue a replacement notice indicating an intention to take further action under paragraph 38 of the Schedule (for example to issue a warrant of distress, which may be a replacement for a warrant previously withdrawn, or to make an attachment of earnings order). Paragraph 37A also allows for an appeal against the replacement notice to be made to the magistrates' court within 10 working days.

487.   Section 88(8) inserts a new paragraph 40A, into Schedule 5 to the Courts Act 2003. Paragraph 40A provides fines officers with the power to withdraw warrants that they have issued, in specified circumstances. A fines officer may withdraw a warrant of control if there is an outstanding sum due and if the fines officer is satisfied that the warrant was issued by mistake (which in this context will include a mistake made in consequence of the non-disclosure or misrepresentation of a material fact).

488.   Section 88(8) also inserts a new paragraph 40B into Schedule 5 to the Courts Act 2003. Paragraph 40B provides magistrates' courts with a power to discharge a distress warrant issued by a fines officer (the court presently has power under section 142(1) of the Magistrates' Court Act 1980 to discharge its own warrant, but not to discharge one issued by a fines officer). If the fines officer has issued a distress warrant and refers the case to the magistrates' court the court may discharge the warrant if there is an outstanding amount to be paid and the power conferred by section 142(1) of the 1980 Act would have been exercisable by the court if the court had issued the warrant. In other words, the court is now able to reopen the case to rectify mistakes, if the distress warrant had been issued by a fines officer, in the same way it can do so if the warrant was issued by the court.

489.   Section 88(8) inserts a new paragraph 40C into Schedule 5 to the Courts Act 2003. Paragraph 40C places duties on fines officers where a warrant of control has been withdrawn or discharged. Where the warrant has been withdrawn by the fines officer or discharged by the court and the court has not discharged a collection order, then the fines officer must take (or retake) one or more of the steps specified in a further steps notice, or deliver a replacement notice and take one or more steps specified in that notice, or refer the case to (or back to) the magistrates' court.

Repeal of uncommenced provisions
Section 89 and Schedule 10: Repeal of sections 181 to 188 of Criminal Justice Act 2003

490.   Section 89(1) repeals those sections of the 2003 Act which would have introduced custody plus and intermittent custody orders for sentences of less than 12 months (sections 181 to 188). Those provisions have never been commenced. Sentences of less than 12 months are now to be brought within Chapter 6 of Part 12 of the 2003 Act: see section 111. Schedule 10 makes amendments which are consequential on the repeal of sections 181 to 188.

Chapter 2: Bail

Section 90 and Schedule 11: Amendment of bail enactments

491.   Section 90 gives effect to Schedule 11 which amends the Bail Act 1976 ("the 1976 Act"), the Bail (Amendment) Act 1993 ("the 1993 Act") and other legislation concerning bail.

492.   The 1976 Act creates a general presumption in favour of bail, both before and after an offender is convicted. This general presumption is subject to certain exceptions which are set out in Schedule 1 to the Act: for example, if the defendant has previously failed to surrender to bail and the court believes that if released he would fail to do so again. Schedule 1 contains a number of Parts which set out the different exceptions that apply depending on whether the person has been accused or convicted of an indictable or summary offence that may or may not be punishable with imprisonment.

493.   The 1993 Act creates a right for the prosecution to appeal to the Crown Court against the decision of a magistrates' court to grant bail to a person charged with or convicted of an offence punishable by imprisonment.

Schedule 11: Amendment of enactments relating to bail

494.   Schedule 11 amends the 1976 Act so that certain of the exceptions to the presumption that bail should be granted to a defendant will not apply where there is no real prospect that the defendant will be sentenced to a custodial sentence if convicted ("the no real prospect test"). This new test (which increases the availability of bail) is limited to non-extradition proceedings and to adult defendants who have not been convicted.

495.   Those aged under 18 will continue to be subject to the existing exceptions in Schedule 1 to the 1976 Act restricting the grant of bail. This is to ensure that those offenders aged under 18 who would otherwise be granted bail under the new test can continue to be given "looked after" status by the local authority (see Chapter 3 of Part 3 of the Act). This means that the young person is assessed by the local authority and receives appropriate assistance and supervision.

496.   Although the new restriction on the exceptions to bail does not apply to under-18s by virtue of this Schedule, a similar restriction on remand to youth detention accommodation is imposed by the youth remand provisions in Chapter 3 of Part 3 of the Act.

497.   Paragraph 5 inserts a new section 3AAA into the 1976 Act which sets out conditions for the imposition of electronic monitoring requirements in respect of children and young people released on bail whilst subject to extradition proceedings. The conditions specified are broadly equivalent to those set out for domestic cases in section 3AA of the same Act.

498.   Paragraph 8 amends section 7 of the 1976 Act which applies to a person who has been released on bail and fails to surrender to custody. In such circumstances the power to remand the person in custody will be subject to the "no real prospect" test, i.e. that there must be a real prospect that the person would be sentenced to a custodial sentence if convicted of the offence. This new test is limited to non-extradition proceedings and to adult defendants who have not been convicted.

499.   Paragraphs 13 and 25 amend Parts 1 and 1A of Schedule 1 to the 1976 Act. These Parts deal with those cases in which the person is accused or convicted of an indictable or a summary offence which is punishable with imprisonment. The effect of the amendments is that certain exceptions to the right to bail do not apply where there is no real prospect of a custodial sentence and the matter relates to non-extradition proceedings and to adult defendants who have not been convicted.

500.   Paragraph 15 amends Part 1 of Schedule 1 to the 1976 Act by inserting a new exception to the right to bail which is not subject to the new 'no real prospect test'. This new exception to bail relates to a person who, if released on bail, might commit an offence involving domestic violence. Paragraph 26 makes equivalent provision for Part 1A of Schedule 1.

501.   Paragraphs 27 to 30 amend Part 2 of Schedule 1 to the 1976 Act, which deals with cases in which a person is accused or convicted of a non-imprisonable offence. The effect of the amendments is to make certain existing exceptions to the right to bail applicable only where the defendant is under the age of 18 or has been convicted of the offence. This has the same effect as the "no real prospect" test in Parts 1 and 1A of Schedule 1 which disapplies certain exceptions to the right to bail.

502.   Schedule 11 also amends the 1993 Act to extend the existing power of appeal so that the prosecution may appeal to the High Court against the decision of a judge of the Crown Court to grant bail to a person charged with or convicted of an imprisonable offence. This new route of appeal is restricted to a decision of a judge of the Crown Court that was not, itself, made on appeal from the magistrates' court under the existing provisions in the 1993 Act.

Chapter 3: Remands of children otherwise than on bail

Remands
Section 91: Remands of children otherwise than on bail
503.   Section 91 is concerned with a child who has not been granted bail and who either (a) has been charged with or convicted of an offence and is awaiting trial or sentence or (b) is the subject of extradition proceedings.

504.   *Subsection (3)* provides that the court must remand that child to local authority accommodation unless one of the sets of conditions set out in sections 98 to 101 is met. (Sections 98 and 99 provide two sets of conditions, one set of which must be met for a child charged with or convicted of a criminal offence; and sections 100 and 101 provide equivalent alternate sets of conditions for children concerned in extradition proceedings).

505.   *Subsection (6)* defines a child as a person under the age of 18. This has the effect of applying these provisions to all under 18s who are before the court in the above circumstances. Currently, 17 year olds are remanded to prison either under section 27 of the Criminal Justice Act 1948 in the case of those charged with or convicted of an offence or the Extradition Act 2003 for those involved in extradition proceedings.

Section 92: Remands to local authority accommodation

506.   Section 92 sets out the practical effect of and arrangements for a remand to local authority accommodation.

507.   *Subsection (4)* provides that a local authority designated by the court must receive the child and provide or arrange suitable accommodation for them. The powers and duties of a local authority to place a child that is remanded under this section are set out in section 22C of the Children Act 1989.

Section 93: Conditions etc on remands to local authority accommodation

508.   *Subsection (1)* of section 93 provides that a court may impose conditions on a child who it has remanded to local authority accommodation. These conditions are the same as the court may apply to a child who is remanded on bail pursuant to section 3 of the Bail Act 1976. *Subsection (3)* also provides that the court may impose requirements on the designated local authority to secure compliance with any of the conditions imposed on the child.

509.   *Subsection (2)* additionally allows the court to order that compliance with any requirements imposed under *subsection (1)* be secured by means of electronic monitoring. In the case of children who are charged with or convicted of an offence the conditions imposed in section 94 must be met. These are same as those which apply to electronic monitoring imposed pursuant to section 3A of the Bail Act 1976. In the case of children concerned in extradition proceedings, the conditions in section 96 must be met.

Section 94: Requirements for electronic monitoring

510.   Section 94 applies in cases other than extradition cases and sets out five requirements that must be satisfied before a court may impose electronic monitoring on a child remanded to local authority care pursuant to section 92.

Section 95: Requirements for electronic monitoring: extradition cases

511.   Section 95 provides for a modified version of the five requirements in section 94 in respect of children concerned in extradition proceedings. The effect of the requirements is broadly the same as for section 94 but the drafting reflects the fact that the child is subject to extradition proceedings in England and Wales.

Section 96: Further provisions about electronic monitoring

512. Section 96 provides that when imposing a condition of electronic monitoring the court must make a person responsible for the monitoring and that they must be of a description specified by the Secretary of State.

513. *Subsection* (2) confers a power on the Secretary of State to prescribe by order the description of persons who may be responsible for electronic monitoring, and *subsection (3)* confers a power to make rules regulating electronic monitoring in general and the functions of the person responsible for carrying out the monitoring in particular. Both the order and the rules must be made by statutory instrument and the rules are subject to the negative resolution procedure in Parliament.

Section 97: Liability to arrest for breaking conditions of remand

514. Section 97 confers a power for a constable to arrest without a warrant a child who the constable has reasonable grounds for suspecting has breached any of the conditions imposed under section 93. It also imposes a duty on the constable to bring the child before a court as soon as reasonably practicable and in any event within 24 hours.

515. If the court determines that the child has broken any of the conditions imposed under the original remand it can remand the child on new conditions or, if it thinks the test for remand to youth detention accommodation is met, remand the child to youth detention accommodation. If it is not satisfied that the conditions have been breached then the child must be remanded to local authority accommodation, again subject to the same conditions as those originally imposed.

Remands to youth detention accommodation

516. A child can be only be remanded to youth detention accommodation under the provisions of this chapter if at least one of four sets of conditions set out in sections 99, 100, 101 or 102 is met.

Section 98: First set of conditions for a remand to youth detention accommodation

517. Section 98 applies to a child charged with or convicted of an offence and describes the first set of conditions that, if met, would allow the court to remand the child to youth detention accommodation. This set of conditions includes a requirement relating to the seriousness of the offence which must be either a violent or sexual offence or one that is punishable if committed by an adult with a sentence of imprisonment of fourteen years or more.

Section 99: Second set of conditions for a remand to youth detention accommodation

518. Section 99 defines an alternative set of conditions that would enable the court to remand a child charged or convicted of an offence to youth detention accommodation. This set of conditions focuses on the behaviour of the offender while on remand. It applies if the child faces a realistic prospect of receiving a custodial sentence. In these circumstances, if they have or are alleged to have committed an offence while on remand in custody and have a recent history of absconding while on remand, or, alternatively, the offence forms part of a recent history of committing imprisonable offences while on remand (on bail or in custody) then they may be remanded securely pursuant to this section.

Section 100: First set of conditions for a remand to youth detention accommodation: extradition cases

519.   Section 100 sets out an equivalent set of conditions to those in Section 98, this time for a child in an extradition case.

Section 101: Second set of conditions for a remand to youth detention accommodation: extradition cases

520.   Section 101 sets out an equivalent set of conditions to those in Section 99, this time for a child in an extradition case.

Section 102: Remands to youth detention accommodation

521.   This section contains general provisions regarding arrangements when a child is remanded to youth detention accommodation.

522.   It provides that the Secretary of State and the Youth Justice Board for England and Wales may direct that the child be placed in a youth detention establishment of one of the kinds in *subsection (2)* namely a secure children's home, a secure training centre, a young offender institution or a new form of youth detention accommodation specified by the Secretary of State pursuant to the existing order-making power in section 107(1)(e) of the Powers of the Criminal Courts (Sentencing) Act 2000.

523.   The Secretary of State, or the Youth Justice Board, must consult the local authority designated by the court before directing where the child must be placed. *Subsection (7)* specifies which authority may be designated.

524.   *Subsections (4) and (5)* make specific provision regarding the giving of reasons and, in the case of the magistrates' court, the recording of reasons for the remand.

Supplementary
Section 103: Arrangements for remands

525.   Section 103 gives the Secretary of State, and the Youth Justice Board, the power to make arrangements for accommodation in a secure children's home for those children who are subject to a remand to youth detention accommodation. Existing legislation enables the Secretary of State to make arrangements for remands to secure training centres and young offender institutions.

526.   *Subsections (2)* and *(6)* give the Secretary of State the power to make regulations (subject to the negative resolution procedure in Parliament) enabling the Secretary of State, the Youth Justice Board or another provider of youth detention accommodation to recover the costs of youth detention accommodation from designated local authorities. It also gives the power to recover associated costs, such as those for providing transport for the child from the court to the chosen form of accommodation.

527.   Conversely, *subsection (4)* gives the Secretary of State the power to make payments to a local authority for the purpose of enabling it to exercise its functions in respect of children who are remanded to local authority accommodation or to make payments in respect of remands to youth detention accommodation.

528.   *Subsection (7)* allows the Secretary of State to provide by regulations that those of his functions that are capable of being exercised concurrently by the Youth Justice Board are to be exercised solely by the Secretary of State either generally or in relation to a particular type of case. Such regulations are subject to the affirmative resolution procedure.

Section 104: Looked after child status

529.   Section 104(1) provides that any child remanded to youth detention accommodation is to be treated as looked after by the designated authority.

530.   *Subsection (2)* gives the Secretary of State the power to apply with modifications or not apply, any legislation (including an Act or Measure of the National Assembly of Wales) to a child who is treated as looked after by virtue of being remanded under this Chapter (children who are remanded to local authority accommodation are treated as looked after by virtue of provisions in the Children Act 1989).

Section 105 and Schedule 12: Minor and consequential amendments

531.   Section 105 gives effect to Schedule 12 which makes various amendments and repeals which are consequential on the new scheme for remands of children otherwise than on bail introduced by Chapter 3 of Part 3.

532.   In general these are very straightforward and involve replacing references to sections of the Children and Young Persons Act 1969 or repealing legislation that created powers and duties associated with remand under that Act. Of note however are:

- *Paragraphs 1 to 3* which amend the Criminal Justice Act 1948. This previously required 17 year olds to be remanded to prison. Under the Act they will be remanded to local authority accommodation or youth detention accommodation.

- *Paragraph 10* which amends section 32 of the Children and Young Persons Act 1969. It has the effect of providing that where a child is remanded to local authority accommodation and they abscond, if found they will be escorted back to local authority accommodation and the cost will be met by that local authority. Where the child is remanded in youth detention accommodation they will be escorted back to youth detention accommodation at the cost of the Secretary of State.

- *Paragraph 13* which inserts a reference to this Act into the Local Authority Social Services Act 1970. The effect of this is to include the functions carried out by local authorities in relation to children remanded to local authority accommodation under the Act in the definition of social services functions for the purposes of the Local Authority Social Services Act 1970. This, in turn, brings children who are remanded to local authority accommodation under the Act into the definition of a 'looked after child' set out in section 22 of the Children Act 1989. In this way a child who is remanded to local authority accommodation under the Act becomes a "looked after child" within the meaning of the Children Act 1989.

Section 106: Regulations under this Chapter

533.   Section 106 specifies which regulations made under Chapter 3 are subject to negative procedure and which are subject to affirmative procedure. Any regulations made under this Chapter may make different provision for different cases and may include supplementary, incidental, transitional, transitory or saving provision.

Section 107: Interpretation of Chapter 3

534.   Section 107 provides definitions of terms used in Chapter 3.

Chapter 4: Release on licence etc

Calculation of days to be served

Section 108: Crediting of periods of remand in custody

535.   Section 108 replaces section 240 of the 2003 Act with a new section 240ZA, dealing with the crediting of time spent on remand in custody against any subsequent sentence of imprisonment or detention. Under section 240 the court directs the amount of remand time to be counted towards a prisoner's sentence. The insertion of section 240ZA provides for such time, instead, to be calculated and applied administratively. All time that meets the criteria of the provision will be counted to reduce a subsequent sentence. There is no longer discretion to disapply any such time.

536.   *Subsection (4)* of new section 240ZA prevents time spent on remand from counting if the prisoner is also serving another sentence or is otherwise detained in connection with another matter *(subsection (10)* lists the types of detention which count for this purpose).

537.   *Subsection (5)* of new section 240ZA prevents the same remand time counting several times against two or more sentences (whether or not they are served consecutively or concurrently).

538.   *Subsection (6)* of new section 240ZA prevents remand time shortening any recall under section 255B where the maximum length of the recall is 28 days. (The possibility of a 28 day fixed recall period was introduced by the 2008 Act which provides that lower risk prisoners who are suitable for such a recall must be released automatically at the end of that period.)

539.   *Subsection (9)* of new section 240ZA makes it clear that consecutive and concurrent sentences, where a prisoner has not been released between serving such sentences, are counted as one sentence for the purposes of deducting remand time. Together with *subsection (5)* of new section 240ZA, this prevents the same remand time counting several times against the overall sentence envelope created by the consecutive or concurrent sentences.

Section 109: Crediting of periods of remand on bail

540.   Section 109 amends section 240A of the 2003 Act which gives the court power to direct that time spent remanded on bail subject to electronic monitoring ("tagged bail") counts towards any subsequent sentence imposed, provided that that sentence is imposed for the same offence for which the defendant was remanded or a related offence. Two days successfully completed on tagged bail count as one day of the sentence. The new provisions set out how the time to be credited has to be calculated.

541. *Subsection (3)* inserts new subsections (3) to (3B) into section 240A. These set out the stages of the calculation. Under Step 1 the first day is counted even if the electronic monitor is not put in place until late that day. However, the last day is not counted if the offender spends the last part of that day in custody: that day will count towards the sentence served.

542. Step 2 prevents credit for tagged bail counting towards a subsequent sentence where during such time on bail the offender was also subject to an electronically monitored curfew requirement in connection with any other sentence (which includes being released on HDC) or temporarily released from prison in relation to another sentence.

543. Under Step 3 days where the offender breached the conditions of the release on bail are not to be counted.

544. Step 4 provides that each day spent on tagged bail effectively counts as half a day against the sentence. If such a calculation results in a number of days that include a half day, that half day can be counted as a whole day under Step 5.

545. New subsection (3A) prevents the same remand time counting several times against two or more sentences (whether or not they are to be served consecutively or concurrently).

546. New subsection (3B) prevents remand time shortening any recall under section 255B where the maximum length of the recall is 28 days (that is, where a prisoner receives the type of 'fixed term recall' introduced by the 2008 Act which provides for automatic release at the end of that 28 day period).

Section 110 and Schedule 13: Amendments consequential on sections 108 and 109

547. Section 110 makes amendments consequential on sections 108 and 109, mainly amending the references to the repealed section 240 of the 2003 Act so as refer to section 240ZA instead.

548. *Subsection (8)* amends section 243 of the 2003 Act in relation to persons extradited to the United Kingdom. For those persons who qualify under section 243 of the 2003 Act, the changes provide for all days remanded in custody in another jurisdiction while awaiting extradition to the United Kingdom to be counted against a subsequent sentence imposed.

549. *Subsection (13)* gives effect to Schedule 13, Part 1 of which replicates in the Armed Forces Act 2006 the effect of the provisions in section 108 for the crediting of remand time towards a subsequent sentence. This ensures the same provisions are applied in respect of sentences imposed under Armed Forces legislation. Part 2 of Schedule 13 makes consequential amendments to other Acts.

Release
Section 111 and Schedule 14: Prisoners serving less than 12 months

550. Section 111 provides for prisoners serving sentences of less than 12 months to be released unconditionally at the half way point. It does so by inserting a new section 243A into the 2003 Act. This replicates the corresponding provision in the Criminal

Justice Act 1991 ("the 1991 Act"). In effect, it replaces the provisions for release of those serving sentences of less than 12 months (section 181: custody plus) originally provided for in the 2003 Act.

551.   Section 111 introduces Schedule 14 which makes consequential amendments in relation to the new section 243A to ensure that the new provision works with the existing release and recall scheme in Chapter 6 of Part 12 of the 2003 Act.

552.   *Paragraph 14* of the Schedule provides that consecutive sentences which add up to 12 months or more are to be treated as a single sentence of 12 months or more. This means that where a sentence of less than 12 months is served consecutively with another sentence and either (i) the other sentence is 12 months or more, or (ii) the two sentences add up to 12 months or more, then release for the sentence of less than 12 months would be on licence for the remainder of the sentence. However, where consecutive sentences add up to less than 12 months, release will be unconditional.

553.   Sentences of less than 12 months were previously all dealt with under the the 1991 Act (by virtue of transitional provisions, this remained the case even after the 2003 Act was brought into force). *Paragraph 17* of the Schedule removes those transitional provisions, so that from the commencement of Chapter 4 such sentences are dealt with under the 2003 Act.

Section 112: Restrictions on early release subject to curfew

554.   Section 112 amends section 246 of the 2003 Act which provides for early release on HDC, which includes electronic monitoring. The amendments exclude a number of categories of prisoner from the HDC scheme. They will prevent anyone serving a sentence of four years or more from being eligible for the scheme. They also make ineligible those previously released and recalled under the scheme for breach of licence conditions (during a previous or current sentence). Also excluded will be those previously returned to prison under section 116 of the PCC(S)A 2000 for committing a further offence before the expiry of a previous sentence. These changes bring the 2003 Act scheme in line with the scheme under the 1991 Act, so that the statutory provisions for HDC will be the same for all prisoners.

555.   *Subsection (5)* inserts a new subsection (4ZA) into section 246 of the 2003 Act. This deals with concurrent and consecutive sentences for the purpose of determining whether an offender is serving a term of 4 years or more.

Further release after recall

Section 113: Cancellation of revocation of licence

556.   Section 113 amends section 254 of the 2003 Act to provide that when prisoners have been recalled erroneously (for example, as a result of incorrect information about the breach), a licence revocation may be cancelled. This will apply even after the Parole Board have considered the recall and made a decision on release.

Section 114: Further release after recall

557.   Section 114 replaces section 255A to 255D of the 2003 Act, which provide for the release of prisoners after recall, with new sections 255A to 255C. There are two different recall schemes under these provisions. Under section 255B prisoners, if not

released executively or by the Parole Board within 28 days, are released at the completion of 28 days detention. Under section 255C prisoners are subject to detention to the end of their sentence unless released executively or by the Parole Board. Section 255A identifies which scheme will apply to a prisoner and sets out the criteria for suitability for automatic release. Recalled prisoners serving extended sentences and those not suitable for automatic release will be dealt with under section 255C.

558.   The changes made by the substituted provisions are as follows:

- The combination of the previous section 255C and 255D allows for the executive release of recalled extended sentence prisoners.

- The re-writing of section 255B removes previous restrictions on automatic release for certain categories of prisoner so that such prisoners may be considered for automatic release if they are assessed as sufficiently low risk and suitable.

- New sections 255B(6) and (7) and 255C(6) and (7) prevent prisoners recalled during their HDC period from being re-released prior to their automatic release date unless satisfactory arrangements for further HDC electronic monitoring can be put in place. These are prisoners who have been released on HDC under section 246 and recalled under section 254.

- New section 255B(8) and (9) allows for the Secretary of State, on receipt of new information, to alter the basis of the recall, so that an offender originally intended for automatic release will be dealt with under the standard release provision (section 255C).

559.   The amendment to section 244(1) of the 2003 Act by *subsection (2)* of section 115 makes it clear that for those serving a sentence of 12 months or more a recall under section 254 can override the automatic release date at the half-way point of the sentence. This means where the 28-day automatic recall period ends after the duty to release at the half-way point under section 244, the full 28 days can be served before release. Similarly, the duty to release at the half-way point will not apply if the Parole Board has not directed release under section 255C.

Other provisions about release
Section 115: Supervision of young offenders after release

560.   Section 115 amends the 2003 Act to include a provision – section 256B – for the supervision of young adult prisoners released from a sentence of Detention in a Young Offenders' Institution ("DYOI") – available for 18 to 20 year olds. This will ensure that prisoners released from a DYOI sentence of less than 12 months will receive 3 months' supervision. This provision recasts a similar provision in section 65 of the 1991 Act, which was repealed by the 2003 Act. Such supervision can include specific requirements relating to drug testing and electronic monitoring.

561.   It also inserts a new section 256C into the 2003 Act to provide for what is to happen if the offender breaches the terms of the supervision. It gives the court powers to summons the offender, issue a warrant of arrest and impose a penalty for the breach.

Section 116: Miscellaneous amendments relating to release and recall

562.   Section 116 makes amendments to the 2003 Act.

563.   *Subsection (2)* removes the duty of the Secretary of State to consult the Parole Board before releasing extended sentence prisoners on compassionate grounds. This brings such release of extended sentence prisoners into line with that of all other determinate sentence prisoners.

564.   *Subsections (5) to (7)* amend sections 260 and 261 of the 2003 Act; these amendments are consequential on the fact that extended sentence prisoners can be removed from prison in order to be removed from the United Kingdom.

565.   *Subsection (8)* corrects a drafting error in section 263(2) of the 2003 Act, which should refer to "section 246" rather than "section 244".

566.   *Subsection (9)* clarifies the previous drafting and practice under the 2003 Act in relation to the duration of the licence period for prisoners released from concurrent sentences. Release cannot take place until the latest release point of all the sentences and is on a licence expiring on the latest end date of all the sentences. No change of policy is being made.

Section 117: Replacement of transitory provisions

567.   Section 117 amends a number of provisions of Chapter 6 of Part 12 of the 2003 Act so that the release provisions of that Chapter apply to sentences of Detention in a Young Offender Institution. This section revokes the 2003 Act (Sentencing) (Transitory Provisions) Order 2005 which had the same effect.

Section 118: Repeal of uncommenced provisions

568.   Section 118 removes various provisions which have not been commenced. One of these is a section of the 2003 Act. Some of them are amendments of that Act or Part 2 of the 1991 Act (which also relates to release and recall).

Life sentence prisoners

Section 119: Removal of prisoners from the United Kingdom

569.   Section 119 inserts two new sections into the Crime (Sentences) Act 1997 to provide a power for the Secretary of State to remove from the UK foreign national prisoners who are serving indeterminate sentences once they have served the minimum term ("tariff") set by the court. The Secretary of State may remove such a prisoner whether or not the Parole Board has directed the prisoner's release. Provision is also made for prisoners who are removed under this power and subsequently return to the UK to be detained in pursuance of their sentence.

570.   New section 32A sets out the criteria for removal and the powers of the Secretary of State to remove a prisoner. This provision applies to those who are removed from prison (whether before initial release or after recall at any time). Subsection (4) allows for release by the Parole Board or compassionate release to apply to the prisoner up until the actual removal from the UK. Subsection (5) imports the definition for a person liable to removal from section 259 of the 2003 Act as it applies for determinate sentence prisoners.

571. New section 32B applies where, after removal, the offender returns. If not initially released by the Parole Board before removal then the offender will be treated as if he had not previously been released. If the Parole Board directed release prior to the removal then the offender will be treated as if recalled for breach of licence. Where the sentence is a life sentence, this will apply at any time until death. Where the sentence is an indeterminate sentence for public protection, then it will apply at any time until the licence ceases to have effect under section 31A.

Application and transitional provision
Section 120: Application and transitional etc provision
572. Section 120 gives effect to Schedule 15 (see below).

Schedule 15: Application of sections 109 to 120 and transitional and transitory provision
573. Schedule 15 contains provision for the application and commencement of the release and recall sections. This provision sets out whether the commencement of the section affects those being sentenced, those recalled or those yet to be initially released after sentence.

574. *Paragraph 4* of Schedule 15 makes it clear that the changes to eligibility for early release on HDC will not affect those who are already released on the scheme prior to the commencement of the changes to section 246 of the 2003 Act.

Section 121: Simplification of existing transitional provisions
575. *Subsection (1)* applies the release and recall provisions of Chapter 6 of Part 12 of the 2003 Act to all prisoners regardless of the date of offence or the date of sentence.

576. *Subsection (2)* provides that provisions relating to the release of fine defaulters and contemnors under Chapter 6 of Part 12 of the 2003 Act will apply to all prisoners regardless of the date of committal.

577. *Subsection (3)* has the effect of repealing fully the release and recall provisions of the 1991 Act and the transitional and savings provisions under Part 2 of Schedule 2 to the 2003 Act (Commencement No 8. and Transitional and Saving Provisions) Order 2005 which saved the relevant release and recall provisions of the 1991 Act. Any 1991 Act provisions needing to be retained for those prisoners in custody at the time of commencement are restated in Schedule 20B of the 2003 Act, which is inserted by Schedule 16 (see below).

578. *Subsection (4)* repeals section 86 of the PCC(S)A 2000, which provides in certain cases for a prisoner's licence to extend to the end of his sentence. Such provision is no longer required for any new releases because section 249 of the 2003 Act will apply; this makes the same provision.

579. *Subsections (5) and (6)* give effect to the Schedules which in effect preserve the provisions which determine the release point and licence length for offenders who were sentenced before 4 April 2005, where the release and licence periods differ from those in Chapter 6 of Part 12 of the 2003 Act.

Schedule 16: Amendments of Criminal Justice Act 2003: transitional and consequential provisions

580. *Paragraph 2 of Schedule 16* inserts a new section 267A into Chapter 6 of Part 12 of the 2003 Act to give effect to new Schedule 20A inserted by *paragraph 3 of Schedule 16*. New Schedule 20A of the 2003 Act makes transitional provision for sentences where the offence was committed before 4 April 2005 where the 2003 Act release provisions will apply,

581. Paragraphs 1 and 2 of Schedule 20A set out definitions for, and the application of, the Schedule.

582. Paragraph 3 of Schedule 20A provides that the old rules for counting days spent in custody before sentence (which included time spent in police custody) continue to have effect, as a modification to the new rule in section 240ZA.

583. Paragraph 4 of Schedule 20A modifies the HDC provisions under the 2003 Act so that those provisions can apply to prisoners who previously fell to be released under the 1991 Act.

584. Paragraph 5 of Schedule 20A provides that those offenders who have been released on licence under the 1991 Act, whether release on ordinary licence, release on HDC, or compassionate release, are to be treated as though they have been released under the 2003 Act provisions. Any specified 1991 Act licence conditions remain valid even where there is no equivalent condition in the 2003 Act.

585. Paragraph 5(6) of Schedule 20A provides that any suspension of the licence by the court under the 1991 Act provision of section 38(2) will continue to apply even though that section has been repealed.

586. Paragraph 5(7) of Schedule 20A provides that any supervision licence issued under section 40A of the 1991 Act (that is, on release from a period of return to custody by the courts in accordance with section 116 of the PCC(S)A 2000) will continue to apply as though it was a licence issued under Chapter 6 of the 2003 Act, but should the conditions of the supervision be breached the offender continues to be liable to be dealt with by the court in accordance with section 40A(4) to (6) of the 1991 Act and not in any other way.

587. Paragraph 5(8) of Schedule 20A ensures that the length of the licence period that would be applicable under the 1991 Act is not affected by treating such persons as though they have been released under the 2003 Act provisions.

588. Paragraph 6 of Schedule 20A provides that where an offender has been recalled under the provisions of the 1991 Act before the commencement date, the recall is to be treated as though it was a recall under the 2003 Act provisions and references to, and decisions of, the Parole Board will be treated accordingly. However, treating the recall under the 2003 Act provisions will not affect the licence lengths and re-release arrangements to which the offender was subject under the 1991 Act. These arrangements have been saved under Schedule 20B and will continue to apply.

589. Paragraph 7 of Schedule 20A ensures that rules made in respect of Added Days awarded on prison adjudications under the 1991 Act provisions have effect if they had been made under the 2003 Act provisions, so that the awarding of added days can be carried forward.

590. Paragraph 8 of Schedule 20A provides that any person removed from prison early for the purposes of removal from the UK under the 1991 Act provisions is to be treated as though they have been removed under the 2003 Act provisions; and that references in the relevant section of the 2003 Act to extended sentences and their relevant custodial periods include section 85 of the PCC(S)A 2000.

591. Paragraph 9 of Schedule 20A provides that any time spent in custody awaiting extradition, awarded by the court under the 1991 Act provisions, is to be treated as having been awarded under the 2003 Act provisions.

592. Paragraph 10 of Schedule 20A defines the custodial period of a 1991 Act extended sentence, imposed in accordance with section 85, as being one half of the custodial term for the purposes of section 264 of the 2003 Act.

593. Paragraph *5 of Schedule 16* amends the 1991 Act to remove the release and recall provisions from Schedule 12 to the 1991 Act in respect of sentences imposed prior to 1 October 1992. These provisions preserve the rules which applied under the Criminal Justice Act 1967 ("the 1967 Act"), the predecessor to the 1991 Act. The relevant provisions are restated in the 2003 Act by virtue of Schedule 20B.

594. Paragraphs *9* to *12 of Schedule 16* amend the Extradition Act 2003 to remove the references to the 1991 Act and make the correct references to the 2003 Act.

595. Paragraph *14 of Schedule 16* amends the 2003 Act to ensure the provisions for crediting time spent remanded on bail whilst subject to an electronically monitored curfew apply to sentences for offences committed prior to 4 April 2005 (in addition to sentences for offences committed on or after that date).

596. Paragraph *15 of Schedule 16* fully repeals the provisions of section 247 of the 2003 Act that require a direction from the Parole Board before extended sentence prisoners may be released between the half way point and the end of the custodial part of their sentence and consequentially removes the saving provisions for that section. The savings for those prisoners who remain subject to Parole Board direction are now provided in Schedule 20B.

597. Paragraph *16 of Schedule 16* removes the provisions of section 262 and Schedule 20 of the 2003 Act which modified the 1991 Act provisions for the those prisoners liable to removal from the United Kingdom. These provisions will no longer be required when all releases are made under the 2003 Act.

598. Paragraph *17 of Schedule 16* amends section 265 of the 2003 Act in respect of the restriction on consecutive sentences for released prisoners by removing subsection (1A). Subsection (1A) applies the restriction set out in subsection (1) to persons convicted of offences committed before 4 April 2005 and to those serving less than 12

months. As the whole of Chapter 6 of Part 12 will now apply to these people, subsection (1A) will no longer be needed.

599.   Paragraphs *18* to *22 of Schedule 16* are consequential on the full repeal of Part 2 of the 1991 Act, removing provisions which amended, saved or made transitional arrangements in respect of that Part.

Schedule 17: Restatement of transitional provision

600.   *Paragraphs 1 to 8* amend various sections in Chapter 6 of Part 12 of the 2003 Act to make clear that those sections are subject to the release, licence and removal provisions of Schedule 20B, which apply to those prisoners who were subject to the release arrangements of the 1991 Act.

601.   *Paragraph 9* inserts new section 267B (modifications of Chapter 6 in certain transitional cases) into the 2003 Act to give effect to Schedule 20B and *paragraph 10* inserts Schedule 20B into the 2003 Act.

602.   Paragraph 1 of Schedule 20B sets out the definitions of the various terms referred to in Schedule 20B and determines that, where an offence has been committed between two dates, the offence is deemed to have been committed on the latest of those dates. Schedule 20B applies to those who were sentenced before the commencement date. For sentences of 12 months or more, excluding offences sentenced under section 85 of the PCC(S)A 2000, the offence would also need to be committed prior to 4 April 2005. However, 2003 Act sentences are defined for the purposes of calculating concurrent and consecutive sentences. Where there are no provisions in Schedule 20B for sentences imposed before the commencement date then the provisions in Chapter 6 of Part 12 will apply unmodified.

603.   Paragraph 2 of Schedule 20B lists the relevant dates when previous legislation brought changes to release and recall arrangements into effect; this explains the reference to such dates in the rest of the Schedule.

604.   Paragraph 3 of Schedule 20B applies the provisions of Part 2 of Schedule 20B to those prisoners subject to:

- 1991 Act sentences
- extended sentences imposed under section 85 of the 2000 Act
- extended sentences imposed under section 227 or 228 of the 2003 Act before 14 July 2008

and disapplies those provisions in respect of those 1991 Act prisoners who have been released on licence from their sentence, recalled, but are unlawfully at large at the date of commencement. Such prisoners, once returned to custody, will no longer retain the 1991 Act re-release arrangements at the three-quarter point of the sentence but will fall to be treated as if recalled under section 254 of the 2003 Act and liable to detention to end of sentence.

605.   Paragraph 4 of Schedule 20B identifies the prisoners still in custody at the point of commencement to whom the release provisions in paragraphs 5 and 6 apply. These are commonly referred to as the DCR (Discretionary Conditional Release) prisoners who were long term prisoners under the 1991 Act and not converted to automatic release at the half way point of sentence.

606.   Paragraph 5 of Schedule 20B applies a duty to automatically release on licence, at the two-thirds point of the sentence, any of those prisoners serving a sentence (or custodial period of an extended sentence) specified in paragraph 4. The duty to release at the two-thirds point applies in place of section 244 of the 2003 Act.

607.   Paragraph 6 of Schedule 20B provides eligibility for release by the Parole Board at one half of the sentence (or one-half of the custodial period of extended sentences) for prisoners falling into the criteria in paragraph 4 (those subject to automatic release on licence at the two thirds point of the sentence under paragraph 5). Paragraph 6 applies the duty to release on the direction of the Parole Board in place of the release provisions of section 244 of the 2003 Act.

608.   Paragraph 7 of Schedule 20B applies to those prisoners serving an extended sentence imposed in accordance with section 85 of the PCC(S)A 2000 who do not fall within paragraph 4. Paragraph 8 of Schedule 20B applies a duty on the Secretary of State to release a person to whom paragraph 7 applies automatically on licence at the half way point of the custodial term. The duty to release at the half- way point is in place of section 243A or section 244 of the 2003 Act.

609.   Paragraph 10 of Schedule 20B provides the duty on the Secretary of State to re-release a prisoner, to whom paragraph 9 applies, unconditionally at the three-quarter point of the sentence. Prisoners to whom paragraph 9 applies are those who were convicted of an offence committed before the Crime and Disorder Act 1998 came into force who have been released and recalled before the changes made by the 2008 Act came into force. This does not include those sentenced under section 86 of the PCC(S)A 2000 as section 86 requires the offender to be on licence to the end of the sentence on initial release and any subsequent release following recall.

610.   Paragraph 12 of Schedule 20B applies the duty on the Secretary of State to re-release a prisoner, to whom paragraph 11 applies, on licence at the three-quarter point of the sentence. Prisoners to whom paragraph 11 applies are those who were convicted of an offence committed after the Crime and Disorder Act 1998 came into force who have been released and recalled before the changes made by the 2008 Act came into force. However, it does not apply to those who have been released and recalled more than once as such prisoners would be liable to detained until the end of sentence in accordance with Chapter 6 of Part 12 of the 2003 Act. Nor does it apply to those prisoners recalled from an extended sentence that had been imposed in accordance with section 85 of the PCC(S)A 2000. Such sentences have their own re-release arrangements in the Schedule.

611.   Paragraph 13 of Schedule 20B identifies the prisoners to whom the release provisions of paragraph 14 apply. These are prisoners in custody at the time of commencement who were sentenced to an extended sentence in accordance with section 85 of the

PCC(S)A 2000 and who were recalled before the changes made by the 2008 Act came into force. It does not apply if the prisoner has been released and recalled more than once as such prisoners would be liable to detained until the end of sentence in accordance with Chapter 6 of Part 12 of the 2003 Act.

612.   Paragraph 14(1) of Schedule 20B applies a duty on the Secretary of State, in respect of those prisoners to whom paragraph 13 applies, where the custodial period of the extended sentence was one of less than 12 months, to release on licence once the prisoner has served the aggregate of half the custodial term plus the extension period. The licence period would thereafter continue to end of sentence.

613.   Paragraph 14(2) of Schedule 20B applies the duty on the Secretary of State, in respect of those prisoners to whom paragraph 13 applies, where the custodial period of the extended sentence was one of 12 months or more, to release on licence once the prisoner has served the aggregate of three-quarters of the custodial term and the extension period. The licence period would thereafter continue to end of sentence.

614.   Paragraph 15 of Schedule 20B provides release provisions for those prisoners serving extended sentences in accordance with section 227 or 228 of the 2003 Act that were imposed before changes made by the 2008 Act came into force. Release is in accordance with section 247 of the 2003 Act at the half way point but only where the Parole Board make a direction for release. Such prisoners are only automatically released once the custodial period has been served providing there has been no recall from licence following earlier release by the Parole Board. This paragraph replaces the transitional provision made when parts of section 247 were repealed by the 2008 Act.

615.   Paragraph 17 of Schedule 20B provides for a licence to remain in force to the three-quarters point of the sentence for those prisoners identified under *paragraph 4* (DCR prisoners) and also to those identified under paragraph 16(2) and (3) – namely, *(i)* those who were short term prisoners under the 1991 Act who have not previously been released from sentence and *(ii)* 1991 Act prisoners serving sentences of 12 months or more who have been released and recalled before changes made by the 2008 Act came into force. Paragraph 16(4) and 16(5) exclude from paragraph 16 those prisoners who have been released and recalled more than once, those prisoners serving a section 85 extended sentence and those where the provisions of section 86 have been applied to the sentence. Section 249 of the 2003 Act (duration of licence) is disapplied unless there is a subsequent recall from licence in accordance with section 254 of that Act.

616.   Paragraph 16(6) of Schedule 20B provides that release on HDC and a subsequent recall for inability to monitor, will not affect the expiry date of the licence at the three-quarter point when the person is re-released at the half way point of the sentence; such a recall does not count under paragraph 16(4) for the purposes of working out whether a prisoner has been released and recalled more than once.

617.   Paragraph 18 of Schedule 20B identifies the prisoners to whom the licence period in paragraph 19 is to apply. These are prisoners serving an extended sentence imposed in accordance with section 85 of the PCC(S)A 2000 where the prisoner has not yet been

released on licence. In accordance with paragraph 19 where the custodial term is less than 12 months, the licence shall expire at the end of the aggregate of half the custodial term and the extension period. However, where the custodial term is one of 12 months or more, the licence shall expire at the end of the aggregate of three-quarters of the custodial term and the extension period. Section 249 of the 2003 Act (duration of licence) is disapplied unless there is a subsequent recall from licence in accordance with section 254 of that Act.

618. Paragraph 20 of Schedule 20B applies the concurrent or consecutive term provisions in paragraphs 21 and 22 to those prisoners serving two or more sentences of imprisonment imposed on or after 1 October 1992 (the commencement of the 1991 Act), where the sentences were imposed at the same time or, where they were imposed at different times but there has been no release from one sentence before the imposition of the next.

619. Paragraph 21 of Schedule 20B provides that where there are two or more sentences and all sentences are 1991 Act sentences, the concurrent and consecutive provisions of the 2003 Act are disapplied because the sentences form a single term with one another. Where one of those sentences is a section 85 extended sentence it is the custodial term of the extended sentence that is used to create the single term. In such a case, the licence period of the single terms is defined by paragraph 21(5).

620. Paragraph 22 of Schedule 20B provides that where there are two or more sentences that are imposed consecutively and some of the sentences are 1991 Act sentences and some are 2003 Act sentences, the sentences are aggregated in accordance with section 264 of the 2003 Act, but the aggregation under section 264 does not affect the length of the custodial period in respect of the 1991 Act sentence. Release does not take place until all the custodial periods relevant to each of the sentences have been served. Paragraph 22 is disapplied where one or more of the concurrent or consecutive sentences is subject to the release provisions of the the 1967 Act; for such cases paragraphs 32 and 33 will apply.

621. Paragraph 23 of Schedule 20B sets out the application of Part 3 of Schedule 20B which applies to those prisoners who are subject to sentences imposed prior to 1 October 1992 ("1967 Act sentences"). But that Part does not apply to prisoners who have been released from a 1967 Act sentence, recalled from licence and are unlawfully at large on the date of commencement. Such prisoners, once returned to custody, will no longer retain the 1967 Act re-release arrangements at the two-thirds point of the sentence but will fall to be treated as if recalled under section 254 of the 2003 Act and liable to detention to end of sentence.

622. Paragraph 25 of Schedule 20B provides for automatic unconditional release at the two-thirds part of the sentence to persons to whom *paragraph 24* applies - 1967 Act prisoners who have not already been released or have been released and recalled before changes made by the 2008 Act came into force. Where a prisoner has served six months or one third of the sentence (whichever is longer) the Parole Board can direct release. These paragraphs do not apply where an extended sentence certificate was issued when the 1967 Act sentence was imposed – release from such sentences is as provided by paragraph 27.

623.   For the purposes of working out whether a person has been recalled paragraph 24(4) provides that release on HDC and a subsequent recall for inability to monitor are to be discounted.

624.   Paragraph 26 of Schedule 20B applies where a person, identified in paragraph 24, is released on licence by the Parole Board. The licence will expire at the two-thirds point of the sentence, provided that there is no recall from licence in accordance with section 254 of the 2003 Act (in which case the provisions of the 2003 Act will apply without modification). Paragraph 26 applies in place of the provisions of section 249 of the 2003 Act in respect of the duration of the licence.

625.   Paragraph 27 of Schedule 20B identifies prisoners who are subject to an extended sentence certificate. Such a certificate extended the licence period to the end of sentence.

626.   Paragraph 28 of Schedule 20B provides for the automatic release of prisoners identified under the criteria of *paragraph 27* after they have served two thirds of their sentence. They will be eligible for release by the Parole Board once they have served six months or one third of the sentence, whichever is longer.

627.   Paragraph 29 of Schedule 20B provides for Prison Rules to be able to provide for the loss of remission awarded against 1967 Act sentences to be treated in the same way as added days awarded against the 1991 Act and the 2003 Act sentences - so that any date on which the offender becomes entitled to or eligible for release and any licence expiry date will be deferred by the number of days so awarded.

628.   Paragraph 30 of Schedule 20B applies the concurrent or consecutive terms provisions in paragraphs 31 to 33 to those prisoners serving two or more sentences of imprisonment where at least one of those sentences is a 1967 Act sentence and either the sentences were imposed at the same time or they were imposed at different times but there has been no release from one sentence before the imposition of the next.

629.   Paragraph 31 of Schedule 20B provides that where there are two or more sentences that are all 1967 Act sentences, the concurrent and consecutive provisions of the 2003 Act are disapplied because the sentences form a single term with one another.

630.   Paragraph 32 of Schedule 20B disapplies the concurrent and consecutive provisions of the 2003 Act where there are concurrent and consecutive sentences where one or more sentence is a 1967 Act sentence and one or more sentence is a 1991 Act sentence, because the sentences form a single term with one another and the single term is treated as though it was a 1967 Act sentence. Where one of the sentences is a section 85 extended sentence, it is the custodial term of the extended sentence that is used to create the single term. In such a case, the licence period of the single term is defined by paragraph 32(5).

631.   Paragraph 32(6) of Schedule 20B provides that where a prisoner is subject to a sentence comprising a 1967 Act sentence, a 1991 Act sentence and a 2003 Act sentence, the 1967 Act sentence and the 1991 Act sentence must be single termed before either the provisions of section 263(2)(c) of the 2003 Act are applied to

determine how long the licence period will be on release or paragraph 33(3) is applied to determine how long the prisoner must remain in custody before being entitled to release.

632. Paragraph 33 of Schedule 20B provides for the treatment of consecutive sentences where one or more of the sentences are 1967 Act sentences and one or more of the sentences are 2003 Act sentences. The Secretary of State cannot release the prisoner until the aggregate of the custodial periods in respect of each sentence have been served. The length of the custodial period that must be served in respect of the 1967 Act sentence is not affected by the application of section 264 of the 2003 Act.

633. Paragraph 34 of Schedule 20B provides that where a prisoner is granted discretionary release by the Parole Board (that is, before any automatic obligation to release), it is the Parole Board who have the responsibility for setting, varying or cancelling any licence conditions. It also provides that where the Board had responsibility for a prisoner's licence conditions before 2 August 2010, that responsibility continues.

634. Paragraph 35 of Schedule 20B provides that a person who is committed to prison before 4 April 2005 for a term of 12 months or more in respect of default of payment of a fine, or for contempt of court, is to be unconditionally released at the two- thirds point of the term.

635. Paragraph 36 of Schedule 20B sets the criteria for application of paragraph 37 - referring to those prisoners who are in custody at the time of commencement, who have passed the half way point of their sentence (or the half way point of the custodial term in respect of those serving extended sentences), but not yet been released.

636. Paragraph 37 provides a power for the Secretary of State in respect of those prisoners identified in paragraph 36, who are liable to removal from the UK, but have not been removed under the Early Removal Scheme, to be removed after the half way point of the sentence (or of the custodial term in the case of extended sentences). The Secretary of State has the power to remove such prisoners with or without a release direction from the Parole Board.

Chapter 5: Dangerous Offenders
Section 122 and Schedules 18 and 19: Life sentence for second listed offence
637. Section 122 inserts a new section 224A (life sentence for second listed offence) into the 2003 Act, together with a new Schedule 15B (which is set out in Schedule 18). Schedule 19 contains related consequential and transitory provision.

638. New section 224A provides that a court must impose a life sentence on a person aged 18 or over who is convicted of an offence listed in Part 1 of Schedule 15B of that Act which is serious enough to justify a sentence of imprisonment of 10 years or more, if that person has *previously* been convicted of an offence listed in any Part of Schedule 15B and was sentenced to imprisonment for life or for a period of 10 years or more in respect of that previous offence. Parts 2 to 4 of new Schedule 15B include offences under legislation which is no longer applicable, offences in other UK jurisdictions and those of other member States of the European Union, as well as offences under service law.

639.   However, the court is not obliged to impose a life sentence where it is of the opinion that there are particular circumstances which relate to the offence, the previous offence or the offender which would make it unjust to do so in all the circumstances.

New section 224A

640.   Subsection (1) of new section 224A sets out the conditions under which the new mandatory life sentence must be imposed. The offender must be an adult when convicted, and the present offence must be listed in Part 1 of Schedule 15B and have been committed after the coming into force of section 224A. The sentence condition and the previous offence condition must also be met (see below).

641.   Subsection (2) of new section 224A gives the court a discretion not to impose the life sentence where it is of the opinion that there are particular circumstances which relate to the offence, the previous offence or the offender, which would make it unjust to do so in all the circumstances.

642.   Subsection (3) of new section 224A sets out the sentence condition. The present offence must be serious enough to justify the imposition of a sentence of imprisonment of 10 years or more. The court must consider what sentence it would have imposed but for section 224A, and disregarding any extension period it would have imposed under new section 226A (which relates to the new extended sentence). This consideration includes, for example, any guilty plea made by the offender, as well as any aggravating or mitigating factors.

643.   Subsection (4) of new section 224A sets out the previous offence condition. The offender must have been previously convicted of an offence listed in any Part of Schedule 15B, and on conviction must have received a relevant life sentence or a relevant determinate sentence.

644.   Subsection (5) of new section 224A sets out what is meant by a relevant life sentence. A relevant life sentence is one where the offender was not eligible for release during the first 5 years of the sentence (not taking into account any period spent on remand or bail). The term 'life sentence' in subsection (5) includes a sentence of imprisonment or detention for public protection (see subsection (10), which refers to the definition of 'life sentence' in section 34 of the Crime (Sentences) Act 1997).

645.   Subsections (6) and (7) of new section 224A set out when an extended sentence (defined in subsection (10), see below) is relevant. An extended sentence is relevant if the custodial term was 10 years or more.

646.   Subsection (8) of new section 224A provides that any other determinate sentence of imprisonment or detention of 10 years or more is a relevant sentence.

647.   Subsection (9) of new section 224A ensures that any reduction of a sentence for the purpose of taking account of time spent on remand, either in custody or on bail, is to be disregarded when considering whether the previous offence condition has been met. It may be that in some jurisdictions where a previous offence might have been

committed time spent on remand is, or may be, applied to reduce the length of the sentence, so the provision deals with that possibility.

648.   Subsection (10) of new section 224A defines "extended sentence" and "life sentence." The definitions include equivalent sentences imposed under the law of Scotland, Northern Ireland and other member States of the European Union.

649.   "Sentence of imprisonment or detention" is defined to include any sentence of a period in custody imposed for an offence.

650.   Subsection (11) of new section 224A provides that offences in respect of which the new mandatory life sentence under that section is imposed are not to be regarded as offences for which the sentence is fixed by law. Among other things, this obliges the court to follow any relevant sentencing legislation when determining the sentence, if it decides that to impose the mandatory life sentence would be unjust.

Section 122(2) and (3) and Schedules 18 and 19

651.   Subsection (2) of section 122 introduces Schedule 18. Schedule 18 inserts new Schedule 15B into the 2003 Act. New Schedule 15B sets out particularly serious sexual and violent offences which are relevant for the purposes of (a) the new life sentence requirements in new section 224A, (b) the extended sentence provisions under new section 226A (see section 124) and (c) the release arrangements under new section 246A for persons serving extended sentences under new sections 226A and 226B (see section 125).

652.   New Schedule 15B contains those offences which are listed in Schedule 15A, which is relevant for the purposes of indeterminate sentences for public protection and extended sentences under section 227 of the 2003 Act and will be repealed. In addition, new Schedule 15B contains certain child sex and terrorism offences as well as the offence of causing or allowing the death of a child or vulnerable adult (under section 5 of the Domestic Violence, Crime and Victims Act 2004). In Part 2, it also includes offences which were abolished before the coming into force of new Schedule 15B, and would, if committed on the relevant day, constitute an offence listed in Part 1 of new Schedule 15B.

653.   Subsection (3) of section 122 introduces Schedule 19. Schedule 19 makes consequential and transitory provisions in respect of new section 224A.

Section 123: Abolition of certain sentences for dangerous offenders

654.   Section 123 repeals provision in sections 225 and 226 of the 2003 Act for sentences of imprisonment for public protection and detention for public protection (the equivalent sentence for persons under 18).

655.   It leaves in place the provision in section 225 which requires life imprisonment to be imposed where the offence for which an offender is convicted carries a maximum sentence of life imprisonment and the court considers the seriousness of the offence justifies a life sentence. It also leaves in place the equivalent provision in section 226 with respect to detention for life.

656.   Section 123 also repeals sections 227 and 228 of the 2003 Act which provide for extended sentences for certain violent or sexual offences (listed in Schedule 15 to that Act).

Section 124: New extended sentences

657.   Section 124 inserts new sections 226A and 226B in the 2003 Act. Those sections create new extended sentences for adults and persons under 18 respectively. The sentences may be imposed in respect of the sexual and violent offences listed in Schedule 15 to the 2003 Act (referred to as "specified offences") where certain conditions are met. For both sentences, the court must consider that the offender presents a substantial risk of causing serious harm through re-offending.

658.   For adults, two further conditions apply as alternatives. Either the court must consider that the current offence is serious enough to merit a determinate sentence of at least 4 years, or at the time the present offence was committed the offender must have previously been convicted of an offence listed in new Schedule 15B.

659.   The second of these alternative conditions does not apply in respect of persons under 18.

660.   Where these conditions are made out, the court may impose an extended period for which the offender is to be subject to a licence (an 'extension period') of up to 5 years for a violent offence and up to 8 years for a sexual offence. Schedule 15 lists violent and sexual offences separately. Specific provision is made about the release on licence of persons serving sentences under these new sections - see section 125 below.

New section 226A

661.   Subsection (1) of new section 226A provides that the new section applies where (a) an offender aged 18 is convicted of a specified offence (whenever that offence was committed); (b) the court considers that the offender presents a significant risk to members of the public of serious harm through the commission by the offender of further specified offences; (c) the court is not obliged to impose a life sentence because of the seriousness of the offence by virtue of section 224A (life sentence for second listed offence) or 225(2) (life sentence for dangerous offenders); and (d) either condition A or condition B is met.

662.   The 'significant risk' test in subsection (1)(b) is the same as the test for indeterminate sentences for public protection, which are abolished by section 123.

663.   Subsection (2) of new section 226A sets out condition A, which is that when the current offence was committed the offender had a previous conviction for an offence listed in Schedule 15B (in relation to the scope of the offences listed there see paragraph 633 above).

664.   Subsection (3) of new section 226A sets out condition B, which is that the current offence is serious enough that, if the court imposed an extended sentence under this section, it would specify an appropriate custodial term of at least 4 years.

665. Subsection (5) of new section 226A sets out the structure of the new extended sentence. It consists of the appropriate custodial term followed by an extension period, which is a further period during which the offender is to be subject to a licence.

666. Subsection (6) of new section 226A provides that the court must determine the custodial term in accordance with section 153(2) of the 2003 Act (provision for length of discretionary custodial sentences).

667. Subsection (7) of new section 226A stipulates that the extension period must be a period of such length as the court considers necessary to protect the public from serious harm caused by the offender's commission of further offences listed in Schedule 15.

668. Subsection (8) of new section 226A sets out the maximum extension periods of 5 years for a violent offence and 8 years for a sexual offence.

669. Subsection (9) of new section 226A stipulates that the appropriate custodial term and the extension period must not together exceed the maximum term of imprisonment that may be imposed for the offence.

670. Subsection (10) of new section 226A follows from the fact that sentences under that section are to be available in respect of offences whenever committed. It allows the court to impose the new extended sentence on an adult offender who has committed an offence which was abolished before 4th April 2005, but which, if committed on the date the offender was convicted, would have constituted a specified offence. And subsection (11) makes section 226A work for offences committed before that date.

New section 226B

671. New section 226B makes similar provision to new section 226A, in respect of persons aged under 18. It contains no equivalent to condition A (see new section 226A(2)).

Section 125 and Schedule 20: New extended sentences: release on licence

672. Section 125 sets out the release arrangements for the new extended sentence (see new sections 226A and 226B, inserted by section 125). Different release arrangements will apply depending on the seriousness of the offence in respect of which the sentence was imposed. Offenders who have committed an offence listed in Parts 1 to 3 of Schedule 15B, or whose offending merits a custodial term of 10 years or more, will be considered for release on licence by the Parole Board once the offender has served two-thirds of the appropriate custodial term, and will be released automatically at the end of the appropriate custodial term if the Parole Board has not already directed release. Offenders who have not committed a Schedule 15B offence but have committed an offence meriting an appropriate custodial term of less than 10 years will be released automatically after two-thirds of the appropriate custodial term.

673. The section also provides for the Parole Board to apply the same release test for the new extended sentence as it currently applies to indeterminate sentences for public protection and life sentences (see section 28 of the Crime (Sentences) Act 1997).

674.   *Subsection (2)* amends section 244 of the 2003 Act to exclude the new extended sentence from the automatic release provisions that apply to other determinate sentences.

675.   *Subsection (3)* of the new section inserts a new section 246A in the 2003 Act (release on licence of prisoners serving extended sentence under section 226A or 226B).

New section 246A

676.   *Subsection (1)* of new section 246A provides that the section applies to a prisoner ("P") who is serving an extended sentence under new section 226A or 226B. It therefore applies to both adults and juveniles.

677.   *Subsection (2)* of new section 246A provides that the Secretary of State must automatically release the prisoner after the requisite custodial period has been served. The requisite custodial period is defined in subsection (8) as two-thirds of the appropriate custodial term. But subsection (2) does not apply where the prisoner's appropriate custodial term is 10 years or more or the sentence was imposed in respect of an offence listed in Parts 1 to 3 of Schedule 15B.

678.   *Subsection (3)* of new section 246A provides that where the prisoner's appropriate custodial term is 10 years or more or the prisoner's sentence was imposed in respect of an offence listed in Parts 1 to 3 of Schedule 15B, the Secretary of State must release the prisoner on licence in accordance with subsections (4) to (7) ., Those provisions provide for the Parole Board to be able to direct release after the requisite custodial period. There is no automatic release until the appropriate custodial term is completed.

679.   *Subsection (4)* of new section 246A provides that the Secretary of State must refer P's case to the Parole Board when the two-thirds point of the appropriate custodial term has been reached. Where the Parole Board declines to direct P's release, the Secretary of State must refer his case to the Parole Board for further consideration at least every 2 years.

680.   *Subsection (5)* of new section 246A provides that the Secretary of State must release the prisoner in accordance with a direction from the Parole Board, provided that the prisoner has reached the two-thirds point of the appropriate custodial term.

681.   *Subsection (6)* of new section 246A sets out the test to be applied by the Parole Board when considering whether to direct a prisoners' release. The test replicates the release test currently applied by the Parole Board to indeterminate sentences for public protection and life prisoners (see section 28 of the Crime (Sentences) Act 1997).

682.   *Subsection (7)* of new section 246A provides for the automatic release of P at the end of the appropriate custodial term where P has not previously been released automatically or released on a direction by the Parole Board. Where P has previously been released and recalled to custody the automatic release provision at the end of the appropriate custodial term will not apply (and P's further release will be dealt with under section 255C of the 2003 Act).

683.   *Subsection (8)* of new section 246A provides that the "appropriate custodial term" means the term imposed by the court as the custodial element of the new extended sentence. This is the sentence imposed by the court excluding the extended licence period. This subsection further defines the "requisite custodial period" as two-thirds of the appropriate custodial term, where a single sentence is imposed. Where a prisoner is serving consecutive or concurrent sentences the requisite custodial term is calculated in accordance with the aggregation of the sentences under sections 263(2) and 264(2).

684.   *Subsection (4)* introduces introduces Schedule20, which makes consequential amendments to the release and recall provisions in Chapter 6 of Part 12 of the 2003 Act. These amendments add references to extended sentence and the new section 246A , so that the appropriate provision in Chapter 6 of Part 12 applies to prisoners released under the new arrangements (for example to allow licences to be set for such offenders and for them to be recalled once released).

Schedule 20: Release of new extended prisoners: consequential provision

685.   *Paragraph 6(3)* (new section 250(5A) of the 2003 Act) provides for the Parole Board to set licence conditions where P is initially released by the Parole Board. Where the prisoner is released automatically the Secretary of State sets the conditions.

686.   *Paragraph 9(2)* (new section 260(2A) of the 2003 Act) provides for the removal of P from prison for the purposes of deportation where P has passed the two-thirds point of the sentence but the Parole Board have not directed release.

687.   *Paragraph 9(4)* (inserting the new subsection (7)(za) in section 260 of the 2003 Act) provides for early removal to apply 270 days prior to the two-thirds point for the new extended sentence, rather than 270 days prior to the half way point as for other determinate sentences.

688.   *Paragraph 10(3)* (new section 261(6)(za) of the 2003 Act) provides for a prisoner who returns to the jurisdiction during the currency of the sentence, after being released from prison early and removed under section 260 of that Act, to be liable to serve the period to the two-thirds point that was not served prior to removal.

689.   *Paragraph 12(2)* ensures that when aggregating consecutive sentences the two-thirds point of the new extended sentence is appropriately calculated.

Section 126: Sections 123 to 125: consequential and transitory provision

690.   Section 126 introduces Schedule 21, which includes provision that is consequential on sections 123, 124 and 125. It also contains transitory provision.

Section 127: dangerous offenders subject to service law

691.   Section 127 introduces Schedule 22, which applies the provision made in Chapter 5 of Part 3 in respect of offenders subject to service law and makes consequential and transitory provision.

Section 128: Power to change test for release on licence of certain prisoners

692.   Section 128 gives the Secretary of State a power to set a release test, or tests, that the Parole Board must apply when considering the release of prisoners serving indeterminate sentences under section 225 or 226 of the 2003 Act (IPP prisoners), prisoners serving extended sentences imposed under section 226A or 226B of that Act and determinate sentence prisoners subject to Parole Board release whose release provisions have been saved under Schedule 20B of the 2003 Act (collectively, "discretionary release prisoners").

693.   *Subsection (1)* gives the Secretary of State a power to make orders setting out when the Parole Board must direct release of discretionary release prisoners. The order may set out either requirements which, if satisfied, mean the Parole Board must direct a prisoner's release or requirements that must be satisfied for release to be refused.

694.   *Subsection (3)* provides that orders can amend the legislation which sets out the release criteria for IPP prisoners, for discretionary release prisoners. Orders may also make provision for prisoners whose case is being considered by the Board at the time when a release test is amended. They may make separate provision for IPP prisoners, extended sentence prisoners and the other determinate sentence prisoners. They may include consequential provision.

695.   *Subsections (4) and (5)* provide that any order made under the section must be made by statutory instrument subject to the affirmative procedure.

696.   *Subsection (6)* defines IPP prisoners and new extended sentence prisoners so as to include both adults and juveniles.

Chapter 6: Prisoners etc
Section 129: Employment in prisons: deductions etc from payments to prisoners

697.   Section 129 makes amendments to the Prison Act 1952 ("the 1952 Act") in respect of the employment and payment of prisoners and persons required to be detained in remand centres, secure training centres and young offender institutions. It makes particular provision in respect of reductions in, deductions from and levies on the earnings of prisoners and persons in young offender institutions who are aged 18 or over.

698.   *Subsection (1)* removes 'employment' from the existing rule-making power in section 47(1) of the 1952 Act. Rules about employment of prisoners and persons in young offender institutions who are aged 18 or over are to be made under the power in new section 47A inserted by *subsection (4)*

699.   *Subsection (2)* amends section 47 of the 1952 Act by inserting new subsection (1A) so that the Secretary of State may continue to make rules about the employment of persons required to be detained in remand centres or secure training centres and persons aged 17 years or younger required to be detained in young offender institutions (see subsection (11)(a)).

700. *Subsection (4)* inserts a new section 47A into the 1952 Act. This confers a number of new powers on the Secretary to State to make prison rules (to which the negative Parliamentary procedure will apply):

- about the employment of prisoners and the making of payments to prisoners in respect of work or other activities undertaken by them (or in respect of their unemployment);

- about the making, by the governor, of reductions in such payments to a prisoner.

- about the ways in which a governor may use the amounts generated by way of reductions – which can be for the benefit of victims or communities, for the purposes of the rehabilitation of offenders, or for other purposes prescribed in rules.

- enabling amounts generated by way of reductions for making payments into an account of a kind to be prescribed. (It is envisaged that such accounts will be for the benefit of the prisoner. The accounts are to be of a kind prescribed in rules, and the rules may also make provision for making payments out of the account to the prisoner before or after the prisoner's release on fulfilment by the prisoner of conditions which are prescribed in rules.);

- to allow for payments of amounts generated by way of reductions to be made after the deduction of amounts of a prescribed description. This is to enable running and administration costs to be taken into account;

- to allow for the making deductions from, or imposing levies on, payments to a prisoner for work, other activities, or in respect of unemployment, where those payments are not made by or on behalf of the governor. It is envisaged that this power will apply in respect of a prisoner's earnings etc. from a range of sources other than the governor;

- to provide for either the governor or the Secretary of State to make deductions or impose levies but that, where the governor does so, the governor must pay amounts generated to the Secretary of State.

701. *Subsections (7) and (8)* of section 129 amend the Prisoners' Earnings Act 1996 to remove its application in England and Wales. It remains applicable in Scotland.

702. *Subsection (12)* gives the Secretary of State a power to make payments in connection with measures that appear to him to be intended to rehabilitate offenders, prevent re-offending or limit the impact of crime.

703. *Subsection (13)* provides that in making such payments, the Secretary of State must have regard to the amounts generated from reductions, deductions and levies made or imposed by virtue of rules under new section 47A.

Section 130: Transfer of prisoners: prosecution of other offences

704.   Section 130 inserts new section 3A into the Repatriation of Prisoners Act 1984. New section 3A will provide prisoners transferred to England, Wales or Scotland, in accordance with international prisoner transfer arrangements, with statutory protection from prosecution in Great Britain in relation to offences committed prior to transfer taking place, except in specified circumstances.

705.   *Subsection (3)* of new section 3A sets out the circumstances in which prisoners transferred to England, Wales or Scotland pursuant to international prisoner transfer arrangements may be prosecuted in Great Britain for offences committed prior to transfer taking place.

Section 131: Transit of prisoners

706.   Section 131 inserts new sections 6A, 6B, 6C and 6D into the Repatriation of Prisoners Act 1984. These new sections will enable the Isle of Man, the Channel Islands or countries with which the UK has prisoner transfer arrangements to transfer, via an airport or port in England, Wales or Scotland, a prisoner serving a sentence of imprisonment to or from a third country, for the purpose of the serving that sentence.

707.   New sections 6A and 6B provide the relevant Minister responsible for executing the transit with the power to hold a prisoner who is in transit through England, Wales or Scotland pursuant to prisoner transfer arrangements for as long is reasonable and necessary to enable the transit to take place. They also provides a power to search a prisoner taken into detention for the purpose of transit. They also confer ancillary powers on the Minster to designate any person as having the powers of a constable for the purpose of executing a transit order and confer a power on a constable or any person so designated with a power to arrest the prisoner without warrant should that prisoner escape or be unlawfully at large.

708.   New section 6C sets out the procedure to be followed where a prisoner enters the United Kingdom through one jurisdiction and exits through another. Transit may only take place in these circumstances where the relevant Minister in each jurisdiction concerned consents to transit.

709.   New section 6D provides a power to detain a prisoner who makes an unscheduled stop in England, Wales or Scotland in the course of being transferred between two other countries or territories, for a period of no more than 72 hours, or until a transit order is issued, as long as the UK has prisoner transfer arrangements with one of those two countries or territories.

Chapter 7: Out of court disposals
Penalty notices
Section 132 and Schedule 23: Penalty notices for disorderly behaviour

710.   Penalty notices for disorder ("PNDs") were introduced by Chapter 1 of Part 1 of the Criminal Justice and Police Act 2001 ("the 2001 Act"). They may be issued where a police officer has reason to believe that a person has committed a "penalty offence", that is one of the offences listed in section 1 of the 2001 Act (which include drunk and disorderly behaviour, possession of cannabis, petty retail theft and causing criminal damage). Recipients of a PND have 21 days either to ask to be tried for the alleged

offence or to pay in full the fixed penalty so as to discharge their liability to be convicted for the penalty offence. Failure to do either of these things may result in the registration of a fine against the individual equal to one and a half times the penalty amount.

711. Section 132 gives effect to Schedule 23, which confers a new power on Chief Officers of Police to set up within their area a scheme which will allow police officers, where appropriate, to issue penalty notices with an education option. This gives recipients the opportunity to discharge their liability to be convicted of the penalty offence by paying for and completing an educational course related to the offence for which the notice was given. An educational course might, for example, seek to make individuals aware of the social and health implications of their conduct and would be designed to reduce the likelihood of further offending.

712. The Schedule also:

- ensures that a PND may not be given to a person under the age of 18;

- removes the requirement that a police officer issuing a PND to an individual other than at a police station must be in uniform; and

- removes the requirement that police officers in a police station may not give a PND unless they are "authorised constables".

713. *Paragraph 3* of the Schedule amends section 2 of the 2001 Act so as to allow a constable to offer an education option to a person given a PND where an educational course scheme which relates to the offence committed has been established by the Chief Officer of the police force concerned. Recipients of a penalty notice with an education option will have the opportunity to discharge their liability to be convicted of the penalty offence by paying for and completing the course. For example, a person suspected of committing the offence of being drunk and disorderly might be offered a penalty notice with an option of paying for and completing an alcohol awareness course instead of paying the penalty amount or asking to be tried.

714. Paragraph 3 also:

- amends section 2 of the 2001 Act so as to prevent PNDs from being given to persons aged under 18;

- repeals section 2(6) to (9) of the 2001 Act which makes provision for the Secretary of State by order (subject to the affirmative Parliamentary procedure) to allow PNDs to be given to persons under the age of 18 but over the age of 10, and to provide for the parents of a person aged under 16 who is given a PND to be informed of the notice and to be liable to pay the penalty; and

- confers a power on the Secretary of State to make regulations (subject to the negative Parliamentary procedure) about the revocation of PNDs.

715.   *Paragraph 3* further amends section 2 of the 2001 Act so as to remove the requirement that:

- a police officer issuing a PND at a location other than a police station must be in uniform;

- a police officer issuing a PND in a police station must be an "authorised constable".

716.   *Paragraph 4* inserts a new section 2A into the "2001 Act". This confers power on the Chief Officer of a police force to establish an educational course scheme in relation to one or more kinds of penalty offence committed in the Chief Officer's area. It stipulates the necessary arrangements a scheme must include; requires that an educational course must aim to reduce the likelihood of the recipient of the penalty notice re-offending; and makes provision about who may provide an education course. It is for the Chief Officer to set the course fee (which must be paid by the person who attends the course). The Chief Officer may arrange for courses to be provided by his or her force, another force, or by a private provider.

717.   New section 2A also:

- allows the Chief Constable of the British Transport Police Force to establish an educational course scheme in relation to penalty offences committed on a railway and other places where that force has jurisdiction; and

- confers power on the Secretary of State by regulations (subject to the negative Parliamentary procedure) to specify the minimum and maximum level of an educational course fee, and allow for the sharing, between the police and those involved in running educational courses, of personal information about an individual who has selected the education option.

718.   *Paragraph 5* amends section 3 of the "2001 Act" (which concerns the amount of the penalty and the form of the penalty notice) in particular:

- to repeal the provision allowing the Secretary of State to specify by order a different level of penalty for persons of different ages (currently £80 for persons aged 18 or over or £50 in the case of person aged under 18 – see S.I. 2002/1837);

- to confer a new power on the Secretary of State by regulations (subject to the negative Parliamentary procedure) to require a penalty notice with an education option to include, or be accompanied by, additional information to that which is provided in a PND without that option.

719.   *Paragraph 6* inserts new subsections (6) to (10) into section 4 of the 2001 Act (which concerns the effect of a penalty notice with an education option).

720.   New subsections (6) to (8) allow for a sum equal to one and a half times the amount of the penalty to be registered as a fine for enforcement against a recipient of a PND with an education option where the recipient:

- fails within a period of 21 days beginning with the date on which the notice was given either to ask to attend an educational course, or to pay the penalty, or ask to be tried for the offence to which the notice relates; or

- asks within that 21 period to attend a course, but then fails to pay the course fee or pays the fee but fails to attend or complete the course in accordance with regulations made under subsection (9).

721.   New subsections (9) and (10) confer a number of new powers on the Secretary of State to make regulations (subject to the negative Parliamentary procedure) in order to make provision:

- as to when an offender will be treated as having attended or not attended a course;

- allowing for extensions of time for attendance on a course (for instance where the offender is unwell) and as to who should determine requests for an extension;

- as to the consequences of the offender failing to attend;

- allowing for the delegation of certain determinations (for instance as to whether extensions of time for completing a course should be granted).

722.   *Paragraph 7* amends section 5 of the 2001 Act so as to prevent a criminal prosecution for a penalty offence being brought against a person given a penalty notice with an education option who:

- asks during the 21 day suspended enforcement period to attend an educational course, unless that person subsequently fails to pay the fee for the course or fails to attend and complete the course; or

- having asked to attend, then pays the fee and completes the course in accordance with regulations made under section 4(9).

723.   *Paragraph 8* allows the Secretary of State to issue guidance about educational course schemes under section 6 of the 2001 Act.

724.   Section 10 of the 2001 Act concerns enforcement of fines registered against a person given a penalty notice who then fails to pay the penalty amount. Subsection (5) allows a magistrates' court to set aside a fine in the interests of justice. *Paragraph 10* of the Schedule inserts a new subsection (7) into section 10. It confers a new power on the Secretary of State to make regulations (subject to the negative Parliamentary procedure) specifying the directions or orders the court may or must give if it sets aside a fine relating to a penalty notice with an education option.

725.   *Paragraph 11* inserts a new section 10A into the 2001 Act. This sets out the Parliamentary procedures relating to any power of the Secretary of State to make orders or regulations under Chapter 1 of Part 1 of the 2001 Act, provides for them to be made by statutory instrument, and confers supplementary powers. New section

10A replaces existing provisions currently found in sections 1(4) and (5), 2(8) and (9) and 3(5) and (6), which are repealed.

726.   *Paragraphs 13 and 14* make amendments consequential upon the repeal of the requirement that constables must be uniform when giving penalty notices, in particular to the Police Reform Act 2002 (which allows for community support officers, accredited persons and accredited inspectors to issue fixed penalty notices).

727.   *Paragraph 15* repeals section 87 of the Anti-social Behaviour Act 2003, which amended section 2 of the 2001 Act so that PNDs could be issued to persons aged under 18 years.

Cautions
Section 133: Conditional cautions: involvement of prosecutors
728.   Section 133 amends sections 22 to 25 of the 2003 Act. The section enables the authorised person (usually a police officer) to make a decision to offer a conditional caution by removing the requirement that, before the authorised person can offer a conditional caution to an offender, they must refer the matter to the relevant prosecutor (usually the Crown Prosecution Service) to decide that there is sufficient evidence to charge the offender with the offence, and that a conditional caution should be given. The section enables those decisions to be taken by the authorised person without reference to the relevant prosecutor.

729.   Section 133 also enables the authorised person to vary conditions in the conditional caution without reference to the relevant prosecutor. The other requirements for a conditional caution remain unchanged, including that the offender admits that they committed the offence and that they consent to being given a conditional caution.

730.   The intention is that the Code of Practice issued under section 25 of the 2003 Act or guidance will specify those matters that should still be referred to the relevant prosecutor for a decision about whether a conditional caution should be given or to vary conditions.

Section 134: Conditional cautions: removal etc of certain foreign offenders
731.   Section 134 amends section 22 of the 2003 Act so as to make available new types of conditions that can be attached to a conditional caution given to an offender who is a foreign national and who does not have leave to enter or remain in the United Kingdom. The object of these conditions is to bring about the departure of the foreign offender from the UK and ensure that they do not return to the UK for a period. These conditions may be attached to a conditional caution, whether or not it is in addition to a condition with one or more of the existing objectives in section 22(3) of the 2003 Act (namely facilitating the rehabilitation of the offender; ensuring that the offender makes reparation for the offence; or punishing the offender).

732.   This section also defines the category of foreign offenders who could be offered such conditions as those offenders whose immigration status makes them liable for removal from the UK. This means a person who has no leave to enter or remain in the UK and in respect of whom there is a power to enforce their departure from the UK.

As with all conditional cautions, the offender must admit the offence and agree to accept the conditional caution.

733.   If the foreign offender does not comply with these conditions he or she may be prosecuted for the original offence.

Youth cautions
Section 135 and Schedule 24: Youth cautions

734.   Section 65 and 66 of the Crime and Disorder Act 1998 ("the 1998 Act") created a system of reprimands and warnings known as the Final Warning Scheme. These are out of court disposals for young offenders for use where prosecution is not in the public interest.

735.   *Subsection (1)* of section 135 repeals sections 65 and 66 of the 1998 Act abolishing the Final Warning Scheme.

736.   *Subsection (2)* inserts new section 66ZA, which creates a new 'youth caution', and new section 66ZB, which sets out the effect of the new youth caution.

737.   New section 66ZA does the following:

738.   *New subsection (1)* sets out the circumstances in which a constable may give a young person a youth caution. They are broadly the same as those in which a warning or reprimand can currently be given. However, unlike reprimands and warnings which cannot be offered if a young person has previously been convicted of an offence or given a youth conditional caution, the new youth caution contains no such restriction. This mirrors changes made to youth conditional cautions (see section 137).

739.   *New subsection (1)(a)* provides that to issue a youth caution the constable must decide that there is sufficient evidence to charge the young person with an offence. The effect of the test is the same as for issuing a reprimand or warning but the wording has been amended for consistency with the requirement for conditional cautions and youth conditional cautions.

740.   *New subsections (2) to (7)* replicate relevant provision from section 65 of the 1998 Act on reprimands and warnings. This includes provision:

- requiring appropriate adults to be present when persons under 17 are given a youth caution,

- requiring the effect of receiving a youth caution to be explained to the person given the caution,

- for the publication of guidance by the Secretary of State, and

- preventing cautions, other than youth cautions and youth conditional cautions, from being given to children and young people.

741.   New section 66ZB does the following:

742.   *New subsection (1)* provides that if a young person receives a youth caution then the police must refer them to the appropriate youth offending team as soon as is practicable. The purpose of this is to ensure that the youth offending team has complete records of the young person's involvement with the police and so that they can be considered for assessment, upon receiving a first or subsequent youth caution. Under section 66 of the 1998 Act this was only required for warnings, not reprimands.

743.   *New subsections (2) and (3)* provide the power for the youth offending team to assess a young person and put in place a rehabilitation programme, where a young person receives a youth caution and they consider this appropriate. It also places a duty on the youth offending team to assess a young person if they receive a second or subsequent referral under subsection (1). Following this assessment, the youth offending team should put in place a rehabilitation programme to prevent further offending unless this is deemed inappropriate. This subsection broadly mirrors the threshold for assessment and intervention that existed for reprimands and warnings.

744.   *New subsection (4)* replicates section 66(3) of the 1998 Act by making provision for the Secretary of State to publish guidance setting out what should be included in any rehabilitation programme and the steps that will need to be taken if the offender fails to participate in these programmes.

745.   *New subsections (5) and (6)* provide that, save for in exceptional circumstances, a court may not conditionally discharge an offender if they have been given a youth caution in the two years preceding the commission of the offence for which they are being sentenced (unless that youth caution was the offender's first and only caution). Where the court is of the opinion that exceptional circumstances are present it must state in open court why it is of that opinion.

746.   *New subsection (7)* replicates section 66(5) of the 1998 Act by making provision that where a young person has received a youth caution and has failed to participate in a rehabilitation programme provided as part of that caution, this may be cited in court in any subsequent criminal proceedings involving that person in the same way that a prior conviction would be.

747.   *Subsection (5)* of section 135 provides that any reprimand or warning given to a person prior to the commencement of this section will subsequently be considered a youth caution for the purposes of the Act. For example a reprimand would be considered a first youth caution for the purposes of determining whether there was a duty on the youth offending team to assess a young person under section 66ZB(2), if they were subsequently to be given a youth caution following the commencement of the Act.

748.   *Subsections (6) and (7)* of section 135 ensure that a referral and rehabilitation programme provided under section 66 of the 1998 Act before the commencement of this section is to be treated as equivalent to a rehabilitation programme provided under section 66ZB of that Act.

Schedule 24: Youth cautions: consequential amendments

749. *Schedule 24* is given effect by section 135(3) and makes various amendments and appeals which are consequential on the repeal of reprimands and warnings under the 1998 Act and the introduction of youth cautions by section 136.

Youth cautions
Section 136: Youth conditional cautions: previous convictions

750. Section 136 omits paragraph (a) from section 66A(1) of the 1998 Act. That paragraph prevents a youth conditional caution from being given to a young person who has previously been convicted of an offence. This will allow a youth conditional caution to be given to a young person when they have admitted to committing an offence for which such a disposal is appropriate, even if they have been convicted of other more serious offences in the past.

Section 137: Youth conditional cautions: references to youth offending teams

751. Section 137 inserts a new subsection (6A) into section 66A of the 1998 Act, the effect of which is to require an authorised person who gives a young person a youth conditional caution to refer that young person to the youth offending team as soon as is practicable. The purpose of this is to ensure that the youth offending team has complete records of the young person's involvement with the police and so that they can be considered for assessment to identify rehabilitative programmes. The referral under this provision will also enable the youth offending team to apply for a "parenting order" if voluntary parenting support is not engaged with (parenting orders are created by section 25 of the Anti-Social Behaviour Act 2003).

Section 138: Youth conditional cautions: involvement of prosecutors

752. Section 138 amends sections 66A, 66B, 66C, 66D and 66G of the Crime and Disorder Act 1998.

753. *Subsection (2)* amends section 66A(4). It removes the requirement that the conditions attached to a youth conditional caution be specified by a relevant prosecutor. A condition that a youth attend at a specified place at specified times may still be attached to a youth conditional caution but the place and times must be specified in that condition by whoever offers the caution.

754. *Subsection (3)* amends section 66B(2). It would allow the decisions as to whether there is sufficient evidence to charge the offender and whether a youth conditional caution should be given to be made by an authorised person. At the moment these decisions have to be taken by a relevant prosecutor (usually the Crown Prosecution Service). The decision taken here is not a charging decision. It is an assessment of the evidence for the purposes of deciding whether to caution only.

755. *Subsection (4)* amends section 66C(5). It removes the requirement that a relevant prosecutor must, if payment of a financial penalty is a condition, specify the amount of the penalty, to whom it must be paid and how it may be paid. Instead, these details must be specified in the condition by whoever offers the caution.

756. *Subsection (5)* amends section 66D. It allows conditions to be varied by any relevant prosecutor or authorised person. At the moment they can only be varied by the

relevant prosecutor. An authorised person will be able to vary the conditions, even where they were initially decided by a relevant prosecutor.

757. *Subsection (6)* amends section 66G, which relates to the code of practice that is issued by the Secretary of State. The amendment is consequential upon the amendment made by subsection (4).

758. The intention is that the Code of Practice introduced under section 66G Act or guidance will specify those matters that should be referred to the relevant prosecutor for a decision about whether a conditional caution should be given or to vary conditions.

Chapter 8: Rehabilitation of Offenders
Section 139: Establishment or alteration of rehabilitation periods

759. Section 139 extends the scope of the Rehabilitation of Offenders Act 1974 so that custodial sentences of up to and including 4 years may become spent. It also inserts new *subsection (2)* into section 5 of the ROA to amend the times at which different sentences may become spent. The table in section 5(2) provides for the following -

   a. Custodial sentences of over 30 months and up to and including 4 years become spent 7 years after the end of the sentence (which would include any licence period). In respect of those under 18 at the date of conviction, those sentences become spent 3 and a half years after the end of the sentence (including any licence period).

   b. Custodial sentences of over 6 months and up to and including 30 months are capable of being spent 4 years after the end of the sentence (including any licence period). In respect of those who are under 18 at the date of conviction, those sentences become spent 2 years after the end of the sentence (including any licence period).

   c. Custodial sentences of up to and including 6 months are capable of being spent 2 years after the end of the sentence (including any licence period). In respect of those under 18 at the date of conviction, those sentences become spent 18 months after the end of the sentence.

   d. Removal from Her Majesty's service becomes spent 12 months after the date of conviction. For those under 18 at the date of conviction the period will be 6 months.

   e. Sentences of service detention become spent 12 months after the day on which the sentence is completed. For those under 18 at the date of conviction the period will be 6 months.

   f. Fines become spent 1 year after the date of conviction. In respect of those under 18 at the date of conviction, they will become spent 6 months after the date of conviction.

   g. Compensation orders become spent when they are paid in full.

   h. Community orders become spent 1 year after the date provided as the end date of the order. In respect of those under 18 at the date of conviction, the equivalent order will become spent 6 months after the end of the date of the order.

   i. Relevant orders become spent on the day provided for in the order as the end date of the order.

760.   Section 139 also inserts new *subsections (3) to (7)* into section 5 of the ROA. *Subsection (3)* provides for a rehabilitation period of 24 months from the date of conviction in relation to any community or youth rehabilitation order which otherwise has no specified end date. *Subsection (4)* allows an absolute discharge, or other sentence not otherwise dealt with in the provisions, to be spent immediately. *Subsection (6)* provides an order making power for the Secretary of State to amend the rehabilitation periods set out in section 5(2) and (3), subject to affirmative procedure. *Subsection (7)* retains the position in relation to consecutive and concurrent terms of imprisonment so that they are treated as a single term for the purpose of calculating rehabilitation periods. *Subsection (8)* defines various terms, relating to the sentences that may be subject to rehabilitation according to section 5 of the ROA. These include references to the armed forces and youth equivalents.

761.   Section 139 also amends section 6 of the ROA which makes provision for when an offender commits a further offence. All rehabilitation periods applicable remain for the duration of the longest rehabilitation period.

762.   Section 139 inserts a new section 8AA into the ROA to deal with spent alternatives to prosecution (a Scottish disposal). The amendment mirrors the law in Scotland so that alternatives to prosecution will be treated in the same way by the law of England and Wales as they are in Scotland.

763.   Paragraph 1 of Schedule 2 to the ROA is amended in relation to cautions and conditional cautions so that they become spent immediately on being administered (cautions) and up to a maximum of 3 months after being administered (conditional cautions).

Section 140: No rehabilitation for certain immigration or nationality purposes

764.   Section 140 relates to immigration and nationality proceedings. It amends the UK Borders Act 2007 to exclude immigration or nationality decision making, including initial decisions and any subsequent proceedings, from the operation of the ROA.

Section 141: Transitional and consequential provision

765.   Section 141 contains the transitional and consequential provisions relating to these amendments. These apply the changes to the ROA retrospectively so that existing convictions will become spent according to the new rehabilitation periods. Anyone treated as rehabilitated for the purpose of the Act before commencement of these provisions will continue to be treated as such. However, the exemption for immigration and nationality decisions will not apply to any proceedings begun but not completed, or applications made but not finally determined, before the commencement of the provisions.

Schedule 25: Rehabilitation of offenders: consequential provision

766.   Schedule 25 is given effect by section 141(10). Part 1 of the Schedule makes minor and technical amendments to the ROA to ensure that the amendments apply to England and Wales only. It also amends the order making power in section 10 of the ROA to give the Secretary of State the power to make incidental, consequential, supplementary, transitional, transitory or savings provisions when making an order under that section.

767. Part 2 of the Schedule makes repeals consequential to the amendments.

Chapter 9: Offences
Section 142 and Schedule 26: Offences of threatening with article with blade or point or offensive weapon in public or in school premises

768. Section 142 creates offences relating to the aggravated use of an offensive weapon or an article with a blade or point, as defined in the offences relating to the possession of such articles under section 1 of the Prevention of Crime Act 1953 ("the 1953 Act") and section 139 of the 1988 Act respectively.

769. *Subsections (1) and (2)* of the section insert the new offences into those Acts to become new section 1A of the 1953 Act and section 139AA of the 1988 Act. The offences are committed where a person (A) has an offensive weapon or an article with a blade or point with him or her and intentionally uses the weapon or article to threaten another (B) creating an immediate risk of serious physical harm to B.

770. A's use of the weapon must be unlawful, allowing A to raise relevant defences to the use such as self-defence, defence of others or property, and the prevention of crime. If raised, the burden of rebutting those defences will rest on the prosecution. "Serious physical harm" is defined as harm which amounts to grievous bodily harm for the purposes of the Offences against the Person Act 1861.

771. Like the offences relating to possession of such articles, the offence must be committed in a public place or on school premises, as defined in relation to the relevant possession offences.

772. The offences under this section will be triable either way, and subject to a maximum penalty of 4 years' imprisonment on indictment. These offences carry a minimum custodial sentence for offenders aged 16 and over. In the case of an offender aged 16 or 17 on the date on which they are convicted, the court must impose a detention and training order of at least 4 months' duration. For those offenders who are over 18, the court must impose a sentence of imprisonment (or detention in a young offenders institution where the offender is aged 18-20) of 6 months. In each instance the court may depart from the specified minimum sentence if there are particular circumstances relating to the offence or offender which would make it unjust to impose such a sentence. In the case of a 16 or 17 year old the court is required to have regard to its duties pursuant to section 44 of the Children and Young Persons Act 1933 when considering whether such circumstances arise. Section 44 imposes on the court a duty to have regard to the welfare of the child.

773. The section also provides expressly that if a person is found not guilty of the new aggravated offence but it is proved that the person committed the relevant possession offence the court can return an alternative verdict of guilty to the possession offence.

774. *Subsection (3)* of section 142 gives effect to Schedule 26 which makes minor and consequential amendments as a result of section 142. The amendment made by paragraph 16 to section 142 of the 2003 Act will allow a court, where a person pleads guilty to the new offences created by section 142, to reduce the sentence of imprisonment it would otherwise have passed; but it may not reduce it to below 80%

of the minimum term referred to in the new section 1A(6) of the 1953 Act and the new section 139AA(8) of the 1988 Act.   The amendments made by paragraphs 23 to 29 to the Armed Forces Act 2006 make equivalent provision in respect of sentencing by a service court to that made in section 142 and Schedule 26 in respect of sentencing by a civilian court. The amendment made by paragraph 30 to the Armed Forces Act 2006 includes in Schedule 2 to that Act an offence under section 42 of that Act as respects which the corresponding offence under the law of England and Wales is an offence under section 1A of the 1953 Act and an offence under section 42 of the 2006 Act as respects which the corresponding offence under the law of England and Wales is an offence under section 139AA of the 1988 Act. Schedule 2 to the Armed Forces Act 2006 lists those serious offences to which section 113 and 116 of the 2006 Act apply.

Section 143 and Schedule 27: Causing serious injury by dangerous driving

775.   This section inserts new section 1A in the Road Traffic Act 1998 ("RTA), and makes provision for a new criminal offence of causing serious injury by dangerous driving. The offence extends to England, Wales and Scotland.

776.   The offence is committed when a person causes serious physical injury to another person by driving a mechanically propelled vehicle dangerously on a road or other public place.

777.   Section 1A (2) defines "serious injury" both for the purposes of England and Wales and in Scotland. In England and Wales, "serious injury" means physical harm which amounts to grievous bodily harm for the purposes of the Offences against the Person Act 1861. In Scotland, "serious injury" means "severe physical injury". The definitions reflect concepts which are familiar in the respective jurisdictions.

778.   Section 1A(3) applies the existing definition of dangerous driving in the RTA to the new offence of causing serious injury by dangerous driving. Section 1A(4) provides that the offence of causing serious injury by dangerous driving only applies to driving after the offence comes into force.

779.   *Subsections (5) and (6)* create an entry in Schedule 2 to the Road Traffic Offenders Act 1988 ("RTOA"), making provision for the section 1A offence to be triable either way and setting out the maximum penalties available on summary conviction (in England this is 6 months' imprisonment or a fine of £5,000, or both; in Scotland this is 12 months' imprisonment or a fine of £10,000, or both) and on indictment (5 years or a fine or both). It also sets out that the offence will be subject to mandatory disqualification and endorsement and sets the range of penalty points available for the offence.

780.   *Subsection (7)* gives effect to Schedule 27, which makes minor and consequential amendments as a result of section 114. Paragraph 1 amends section 13A(1) of the "RTA" so that the new offence does not apply to motoring events authorised under regulations made by the Secretary of State under that section.

781.   Paragraphs 2 to 4 amend sections 23 and 24 of the RTOA to provide for alternative verdicts.   Where a person is found not guilty of culpable homicide in Scotland, or

manslaughter in England and Wales, they may instead be convicted of the new offence. A person found not guilty of the new offence may in the alternative be convicted of dangerous driving (contrary to section 2 of the RTA) or careless, or inconsiderate, driving (contrary to section 3 of the RTA).

782. Paragraphs 5 and 6 amend sections 34(4) and 36(2)(b) of the RTOA to make provision in respect of disqualification. A person convicted of the new offence will be subject to a minimum disqualification of two years, unless the court considers there are special reasons either not to disqualify them, or to disqualify for a shorter period. A person convicted of the new offence will be disqualified until they pass an extended driving test (section 36 of the RTOA).

783. Paragraphs 7 and 8 amend section 45(6) and, prospectively, section 45A(4) of the RTOA so that an endorsement in relation to the new offence will remain effective until four years have elapsed following conviction. Paragraph 9 inserts the new offence into Schedule 1 to the RTOA for the purpose of applying sections 11 and 12(1) of that Act relating to evidence as to driver, user or owner of a vehicle in proceedings in England and Wales.

784. Paragraph 10 amends, prospectively, paragraph 3 of Schedule 3 to the Crime (International Co-operation) Act 2003 to insert the new offence. Where a defendant is normally resident outside the UK, notice of conviction and disqualification for the new offence will be given to the authorities of a state where they are normally resident.

785. Paragraph 11 amends Schedule 2 to the Armed Forces Act 2006 to insert the new offence into that Schedule for the purpose of sections 113 and 116 of that Act. Those sections govern the reporting of serious offences to the service police force and the Director of Service Prosecutions respectively.

Section 144: Offence of squatting in a residential building
786. This section creates a new offence of squatting in a residential building.

787. *Subsection (1)* sets out the elements of the offence. The offence is committed when a person is in a residential building as a trespasser having entered it as such, the person knows or ought to know that they are a trespasser, and the person is living in the building or intends to live there for any period.

788. *Subsection (1)(a)* is designed to ensure that only people who enter and remain in the residential building as trespasser will be captured by the offence. It will not cover anybody who entered the building with permission of the property owner, such as a legitimate tenant.

789. *Subsection (1)(b)* states that the offence will only be committed if the defendant knew or ought to have known he or she was a trespasser.

790. *Subsection (1)(c)* provides that the trespasser must be living or intending to live in the building for any period. The offence does not apply to people who are in the residential building momentarily or have no intention of living there.

791.   *Subsection (2)* is designed to ensure that the offence is not committed by a person who remains in occupation after the end of a lease or licence.

792.   'Residential building' is defined in *subsection (3)*.

793.   *Subsection (4)* makes it clear that a defendant who occupied a residential building with the permission (e.g. consent or licence) of a trespasser can, where appropriate, still be considered a trespasser as against the owner or lawful occupier and as such be captured by the offence.

794.   The offence will be triable summarily only and will carry a maximum penalty of six months' imprisonment, a level 5 fine or both. The maximum penalty of imprisonment will become 51 weeks if section 281(5) of the 2003 Act is commenced.

795.   *Subsection (7)* provides that the offence applies regardless of whether the trespasser entered the property before or after commencement of the section. The offence will therefore apply if having entered the building as a trespasser the person commits the following elements after commencement of the section: they are in the building as a trespasser; they know or ought to know that they are a trespasser, and they are living in the building or intend to live there.

796.   *Subsection (8)* amends section 17 of the Police and Criminal Evidence Act 1984 to give uniformed police officers the power to enter and search premises for the purpose of arresting a person for the offence of squatting in a residential building.

797.   *Subsection (9)* makes a consequential amendment to Schedule 10 to the Criminal Justice and Public Order Act 1994 by removing a reference to a previous amendment to section 17(3) of the Police and Criminal Evidence Act 1984.

Section 145: Scrap metal dealing: increase in penalties for existing offences

798.   Section 145 raises the level of fines available for certain offences under the Scrap Metal Dealers Act 1964, which regulates those carrying on business as a scrap metal dealer. The effect of the section is to increase the level of fine available for those offences by two levels on the standard scale.

Section 146: Offence of buying scrap metal for cash etc

799.   Section 146(2) inserts new section 3A into the Scrap Metal Dealers Act 1964 ("the Act") creating a criminal offence of buying scrap metal for cash etc.

800.   The new section 3A prohibits scrap metal dealers paying for scrap metal other than by cheque or by electronic transfer. For the purpose of the offence, "paying" includes payments in kind using goods or services. Section 3A(2) gives the Secretary of State a power, by order (subject to the affirmative Parliamentary procedure), to permit other methods of payment. The offence does not apply if the payment was made in the carrying on of the dealer's business as a scrap metal dealer as part of the business of an itinerant collector and, at the time of the payment, an order by the local authority was in force in accordance with section 3(1) of the Act is in force. A person guilty of the offence is liable on summary conviction to a fine not exceeding level 5 on the standard scale.

801.   *Subsections (3) to (12)* make consequential amendments to the record-keeping requirements under sections 2 and 3 of the Act. These amendments include a requirement for the dealer to record the method of payment and keep a copy of any cheque or any receipt identifying the transfer. The record-keeping provisions referred to do not apply to itinerant collectors who have an order from the relevant local authority under section 3(1) of the Act.

802.   *Subsection (14)* amends section 6 of the Act to provide a constable with a right of entry, exercisable by warrant, to a scrap metal store where scrap metal paid for contrary to the prohibition on cash payments has been received or kept, or to a place to which admission is reasonably required to ascertain whether the prohibition on cash payments is being complied with.

Section 147: Review of offence of buying scrap metal for cash etc

803.   Section 147 places a duty on the Secretary of State to review the offence of buying scrap metal for cash within five years of the offence coming into force. The purpose of this review is to assess whether the offence has achieved the objectives that it was intended to achieve and whether it is appropriate to retain the offence.

Section 148: Reasonable force for the purposes of self-defence etc

804.   Section 148 amends section 76 of the 2008 Act, which provides a gloss on the common law of self-defence and the defences provided by section 3(1) of the Criminal Law Act 1967 and section 3(1) of the Criminal Law Act (Northern Ireland) 1967.

805.   These amendments expand section 76 so that the law relating to self-defence and related defences is set out clearly in one place.

806.   *Subsection (2)* expands the list of defences in section 76(2) of the 2008 Act to include the common law defence of defence of property.

807.   *Subsection (3)* adds a new subsection (6A) to section 76 of the 2008 Act. This is designed to make clear the existing legal position that a person is not under a duty to retreat but the possibility that they could have retreated is an element in the consideration of whether the degree of force used by that person was reasonable in all the circumstances as that person believed them to be.

808.   *Subsection (4)* amends subsection 76(8) of the 2008 Act to make it clear that the new subsection (6A) does not prevent other matters from being taken into consideration when the court is deciding whether the degree of force used by the defendant was reasonable in the circumstances.

809.   *Subsection (5)* amends subsection (10)(a) of the 2008 Act which defines the meaning of "legitimate purpose" for the purpose of section 76 of the 2008 Act. The amendment provides that a legitimate purpose includes the defence of property under common law.

810.   *Subsection (6)* ensures that the amendments to section 76 of the 2008 Act will apply whether the alleged offence took place before, or on or after, the date on which the amendments come into force. The amendments will not apply, however, in relation to a trial on indictment or any proceedings in respect of that trial where the arraignment took place before the date on which the amendments come into force, nor will they apply to a summary trial or any proceedings in respect of that trial which began before the commencement date. Similar transitional provision applies where the alleged offence is a service offence.

811.   The amendments to section 76 of the 2008 Act and the transitional provision in *subsection (6)* will extend to England and Wales only though, in relation to service offences, the amendments and transitional provision also extend to Scotland and Northern Ireland. The remaining provisions of section 76 of the 2008 Act will continue to extend to England and Wales and Northern Ireland (and, in relation to service offences, Scotland).

Part 4: Final provisions
Section 149: Power to make consequential and supplementary provision etc
812.   Section 149 gives the Lord Chancellor and the Secretary of State a power to make consequential, supplementary, incidental, transitional, transitory or saving provision by regulations in relation to any provision in the Act. Such provision may amend, repeal, revoke or otherwise modify Acts of Parliament and Acts or Measures of the National Assembly for Wales passed before or in the same Session as the Act and instruments made under such Acts or Measures before the provision in question comes into force.

813.   *Subsections (4) and (5)* provide that, where the regulations amend or repeal an Act of Parliament or an Act or Measure of the National Assembly for Wales, they will be subject to the affirmative resolution procedure. Otherwise, the regulations will be subject to the negative resolution procedure

Section 151: Commencement
814.   Section 151 makes provision for commencement of the Act. Sections 77 (piloting of alcohol abstinence and monitoring requirements) and 119 (removal of prisoners from the United Kingdom) and Part 4 of the Act come into force on Royal Assent. The remainder of the Act will be commenced by order made by the Lord Chancellor or the Secretary of State.

Section 152: Extent
815.   Section 152 sets out the extent of the provisions, details of which are set out at paragraphs 53 to 60.

Section 153: Channel Islands, Isle of Man and British overseas territories
816.   Section 153 provides that, where the Act amends certain Acts which may be extended to the Channel Islands, Isle of Man and British overseas territories, the amendments made by the Act may also be extended to those jurisdictions.

hansard references

817.   The following table sets out the dates and Hansard references for each stage of this Act's passage through Parliament.

Stage	Date	Hansard Reference
House of Commons		
Introduction	21 June 2011	Vol. 530 Col 192
Second Reading	29 June 2011	Vol. 530 Col 984
Committee	12 July 2011	Legal Aid, Sentencing & Punishment of Offenders Bill Committee
	14 July 2011	
	19 July 2011	
	6 September 2011	
	8 September 2011	
	13 September 2011	
	15 September 2011	
	11 October 2011	
	13 October 2011	
Report	31 October 2011	Vol. 534 Col 633
	1 November 2011	Vol. 534 Col 784
Report and Third Reading	2 November 2011	Vol. 534 Col 1951
House of Lords		
Introduction	3 November 2011	Vol. 731 Col 1349
Second Reading	21 November 2011	Vol. 732 Col 821
Committee	20 December 2011	Vol. 733 Col 1688
	10 January 2012	Vol. 734 Col 12
	16 January 2012	Vol. 734 Col 348
	18 January 2012	Vol. 734 Col 582
	24 January 2012	Vol. 734 Col 928
	30 January 2012	Vol. 734 Col 1331
	1 February 2012	Vol. 734 Col 1573
	7 February 2012	Vol. 735 Col 131
	9 February 2012	Vol. 735 Col 370
	15 February 2012	Vol. 735 Col 864

Stage	Date	Hansard Reference
Report	5 March 2012	Vol. 735 Col 1559
	7 March 2012	Vol. 735 Col 1782
	12 March 2012	Vol. 736 Col 69
	14 March 2012	Vol. 736 Col 279
	20 March 2012	Vol. 736 Col 752
Third Reading	27 March 2012	Vol. 736 Col 1253
Commons Consideration of Lords Amendments	17 April 2012	Vol. 543 Col 195
Lords Consideration of Commons Reasons and Amendment	23 April 2012	Vol. 736 Col 1557
Commons Consideration of Lords Message	24 April 2012	Vol. 543 Col 830
Lords Consideration of Commons Reason	25 April 2012	Vol. 736 Col 1796
Royal Assent	1 May 2012	Vol. 736 Col 2114 Vol. 543 Col 1371

ANNEX A

Table of abbreviations used in the explanatory notes.

Abbreviation	Meaning
"the 2003 Act"	Criminal Justice Act 2003
"PCC(S)A 2000"	Powers of Criminal Courts (Sentencing) Act 2000
"LSC"	Legal Services Commission
"CFA"	Conditional Fee Agreements
"the Director"	Director of Legal Aid Casework
"HDC"	Home Detention Curfew
"DYOI"	Detention in Young Offenders Institution
"the 1991 Act"	Criminal Justice Act 1991
"the 1967 Act"	Criminal Justice Act 1967
"the POA 1985"	Prosecution of Offences Act 1985
"DCO"	Defendant's costs order
"CMC"	Claim Management Companies
"the 1973 Act"	Matrimonial Causes Act 1973
"ATE insurance"	After the Event Insurance
"DBA"	Damages Based Agreements
"the ROA"	Rehabilitation of Offenders Act 1974
"DTO"	Detention and Training Order
"IPP prisoners"	Indeterminate Sentence for Public Protection
"the 2008 Act"	Criminal Justice and Immigration Act 2008

Abbreviation	Meaning
"the 1952 Act"	Prison Act 1952
"PND"	Penalty Notices for Disorder
"the 2001 Act"	Criminal Justice and Police Act 2001
"the 1998 Act"	Crime and Disorder Act 1998
"the 1953 Act"	Prevention of Crime Act 1953
"the 1988 Act"	Criminal Justice Act 1988
"RTA"	Road Traffic Act 1988
"RTOA"	Road Traffic Offenders Act 1988
"the 1993 Act"	Bail (Amendment) Act 1993
"the 1976 Act"	Bail Act 1976

ANNEX B

Table of contents for Schedule 1

818.   Part 1 of Schedule 1 provides descriptions in each area of law for which civil legal aid services may be made available. Each description includes any applicable conditions and refers to the exclusions in Part 2 and Part 3 that apply as well as, in some cases, making further specific exclusions.

819.   The exclusion of advocacy in Part 3 applies to all of the paragraphs of Part 1 with the exception of cross-border disputes (see paragraph 44 of Part 1). In relation to connected matters (see paragraph 46 of Part 1) the exclusions in Part 2 and Part 3 apply except to the extent that regulations prescribe otherwise. Part 3 is explained at paragraph 100 above.

820.   The table below summarises which exclusions (other than the exclusion in Part 3) apply in relation to each paragraph of Part 1 of Schedule 1.

Part 1 –paragraph number	Part 2 and other exclusions that apply
P1 Care, supervision and protection of children	All Part 2 exclusions.
P2 Special educational needs	All Part 2 exclusions.
P3 Abuse of child or vulnerable adult	All Part 2 exclusions except: personal injury or death, a claim in tort in respect of negligence, a claim in tort in respect of assault, battery or false imprisonment, a claim in tort in respect of breach of statutory duty, and a damages claim for breach of Convention rights made in reliance on section 7 of the Human Rights Act 1998. Exclusion in relation to clinical negligence. Exclusion in relation to services provided in relation to a matter arising under a family enactment (defined in paragraph 12).
P4 Working with children and vulnerable adults	All Part 2 exclusions.
P5 Mental health and mental capacity	All Part 2 exclusions.

Part 1 –paragraph number	Part 2 and other exclusions that apply
	Exclusions in relation to creation of lasting powers of attorney and making of advance decisions under the Mental Capacity Act 2005.
P6 Community care	All Part 2 exclusions.
P7 Facilities for disabled persons	All Part 2 exclusions.
P8 Appeals relating to welfare benefits	All Part 2 exclusions except personal injury or death and civil legal services in relation to a benefit, allowance, payment, credit or pension under certain enactments.
P9 Inherent jurisdiction of High Court in relation to children and vulnerable adults	All Part 2 exclusions.
P10 Unlawful removal of children	All Part 2 exclusions.
P11 Family homes and domestic violence	All Part 2 exclusions except a claim in tort in respect of assault, battery or false imprisonment and trust law.
P12 Victims of domestic violence and family matters	All Part 2 exclusions except trust law. Exclusion of services provided in relation to a claim in tort relating to domestic violence. Services that may be provided include conveyancing in some circumstances.
P13 Protection of children and family matters	All Part 2 exclusions.
P14 Mediation in family disputes	All Part 2 exclusions except trust law. Services that may be provided include conveyancing in some circumstances.

Part 1 –paragraph number	Part 2 and other exclusions that apply
P15 Children who are parties to family proceedings	All Part 2 exclusions.
P16 Forced marriage	All Part 2 exclusions.
P17 EU and international agreements concerning children	All Part 2 exclusions.
P18 EU and international agreements concerning maintenance	All Part 2 exclusions except trust law.
P19 Judicial review	All Part 2 exclusions except personal injury or death, a claim in tort in respect of negligence, a claim in tort in respect of assault, battery or false imprisonment, a claim in tort in respect of trespass to goods, a claim in tort in respect of trespass to land, damage to property, a claim in tort in respect of breach of statutory duty, a damages claim for breach of Convention rights made in reliance on section 7 of the Human Rights Act 1998, civil legal services in relation to a benefit, allowance, payment, credit or pension under certain enactments and compensation under the Criminal Injuries Compensation Scheme. Exclusion in relation to judicial reviews that do not have the potential to produce a benefit for the individual, a member of the individual's family or the environment. Exclusion in relation to certain immigration cases and exceptions to those exclusions.
P20 Habeas corpus	All Part 2 exclusions.
P21 Abuse of position or powers by public authority	All Part 2 exclusions except personal injury or death, claim in tort in respect of negligence, a claim

Part 1 –paragraph number	Part 2 and other exclusions that apply
	in tort in respect of assault, battery or false imprisonment, a claim in tort in respect of trespass to goods, a claim in tort in respect of trespass to land, damage to property, a claim in tort in respect of breach of statutory duty and a damages claim for breach of Convention rights made in reliance on section 7 of the Human Rights Act 1998. Exclusion in relation to clinical negligence.
P22 Breach of Convention rights by public authority	All Part 2 exclusions except personal injury or death, claim in tort in respect of negligence, a claim in tort in respect of assault, battery or false imprisonment, a claim in tort in respect of trespass to goods, a claim in tort in respect of trespass to land, damage to property, a claim in tort in respect of breach of statutory duty and a damages claim for breach of Convention rights made in reliance on section 7 of the Human Rights Act 1998. Exclusion in relation to clinical negligence.
P23 Clinical negligence and severely disabled infants	All Part 2 exclusions except personal injury or death, a claim in tort in respect of negligence, a claim in tort in respect of assault, battery or false imprisonment, and a claim in tort in respect of breach of statutory duty.
P24 Special Immigration Appeals Commission	All Part 2 exclusions.
P25 Immigration: detention	All Part 2 exclusions.
P26 Immigration: temporary admission	All Part 2 exclusions.

Part 1 –paragraph number	Part 2 and other exclusions that apply
P27 Immigration: residence etc restrictions	All Part 2 exclusions.
P28: Immigration: victims of domestic violence and indefinite leave to remain	All Part 2 exclusions. Exclusion in relation to attendance at an interview
P29 Immigration: victims of domestic violence and residence cards	All Part 2 exclusions. Exclusion in relation to attendance at an interview.
P30 Immigration: rights to enter and remain	All Part 2 exclusions. Exclusion in relation to attendance at an interview.
P31 Immigration: accommodation for asylum seekers etc	All Part 2 exclusions.
P 32 Victims of trafficking in human beings	For civil legal services provided in relation to applications for leave to enter, or to remain in, the UK - All Part 2 exclusions. For civil legal services provided in relation to employment law or damages claims – All Part 2 exclusions except personal injury or death, a claim in tort in respect of negligence, a claim in tort in respect of assault, battery or false imprisonment, a claim in tort in respect of trespass to goods, a claim in tort in respect of trespass to land, damage to property, and a claim in tort in respect of breach of statutory duty.
P33 Loss of home	All Part 2 exclusions except business. Exception from those exclusions for certain applications under the Trusts of Land and Appointment of

Part 1 –paragraph number	Part 2 and other exclusions that apply
	Trustees Act 1996 in connection with bankruptcy. Exception from the Part 2 exclusions for a claim in tort in respect of assault, battery or false imprisonment, a claim in tort in respect of trespass to goods, a claim in tort in respect of trespass to land, damage to property and a claim in tort in respect of breach of statutory duty in respect of counterclaims in possession/sale proceedings and unlawful eviction. Exclusion in relation to certain proceedings under the Matrimonial Causes Act 1973 and the Civil Partnership Act 2004
P34 Homelessness	All Part 2 exclusions.
P35 Risk to health or safety in rented home	All Part 2 exclusions except damage to property and a claim in tort in respect of breach of statutory duty.
P36 Anti-social behaviour	All Part 2 exclusions.
P37 Protection from harassment	All Part 2 exclusions.
P38 Gang related violence	All Part 2 exclusions.
P39 Sexual offences	All Part 2 exclusions except personal injury or death, a claim in tort in respect of negligence, assault, battery or false imprisonment, a claim in tort in respect of breach of statutory duty, damages claims for breach of Convention rights.
P40 Proceeds of crime	All Part 2 exclusions except business. Specific exclusions in connection

Part 1 –paragraph number	Part 2 and other exclusions that apply
	with confiscation orders.
P41 Inquests	All Part 2 exclusions except personal injury or death.
P42 Environmental pollution	All Part 2 exclusions.
P43 Equality	All Part 2 exclusions except civil legal services in relation to a benefit, allowance, payment, credit or pension under certain enactments.
P44 Cross-border disputes	Not subject to the exclusions in Part 2.
P45 Terrorism prevention and investigation measures etc	All Part 2 exclusions.
P46 Connected matters	All Part 2 exclusions except to the extent that regulations provide otherwise.

ANNEX C

Detailed explanatory note for Part 1 of Schedule 1

Paragraph 1: Care, supervision and protection of children

821. *Paragraph 1* brings within scope civil legal services in relation to certain orders and proceedings relating to the intervention of a local authority in the care, supervision and protection of a child.

822. *Paragraph 1(1)* lists the types of cases involving care, supervision and protection of children that are to be within scope. These include where the local authority is considering commencing, or has commenced, care or supervision proceedings under Part IV of the Children Act 1989 in respect of a child, proceedings for a child assessment order or proceedings for an emergency protection order under Part V of the Children Act 1989, and adoption cases under the Adoption and Children Act 2002. So, for example, legal aid will be available for parents where a local authority is seeking to take their child into care.

823. *Paragraph 1(2)* brings within the scope of civil legal aid services for cases related to those set out at paragraph 1(1); that is, where an order is sought as an alternative to one of those orders, or for proceedings heard together with proceedings relating to such an order. So, for example, an application for a special guardianship order in respect of a child who is the subject of a care order application by a local authority will be in scope, if the two proceedings are to be heard together or the special guardianship order is an alternative to the care order.

Paragraph 2: Special educational needs

824. *Paragraph 2(1)(a)* brings within the scope of civil legal aid matters arising under Part 4 of the Education Act 1996. These are typically challenges relating to a local education authority's assessment of a child's special educational needs.

825. *Paragraph 2(1)(b)* brings within scope civil legal services for cases relating to Learning Difficulty Assessments under sections 139A and 140 of the Learning and Skills Act 2000. This will allow funding for special educational needs cases for persons aged between 16 and 24.

826. *Paragraph 2(2)* applies the exclusions in Part 2 and the advocacy exclusion in Part 3. Legal aid in the form of advocacy may be made available for appeals in the Upper Tribunal on a point of law from decisions made by the First-tier (Special Educational Needs and Disability – SEND) Tribunal or the Special Educational Needs Tribunal for Wales under Part 4 of the Education Act 1996 (see paragraph 17 of Part 3 of Schedule 1).

Paragraph 3: Abuse of child or vulnerable adult

827.   This paragraph brings within the scope of civil legal aid services provided in relation to the abuse of an individual that took place when the individual was a child or vulnerable adult. Such services are within the scope of civil legal aid if they are provided to the individual concerned. They are also within the scope of civil legal aid if the individual concerned has died and the services are provided to the individual's personal representative or for the purposes of a claim under the Fatal Accidents Act 1976 for the benefit of the individual's dependants. This will include services provided in relation to claims by individuals who allege abuse in local authority care, and claims against a local authority for failure to take an individual into care. This paragraph will also include claims against the alleged perpetrator of abuse.

828.   *Sub-paragraph (2)(a)* applies the exclusions in Part 2 except in relation to personal injury or death, a claim in tort in respect of negligence, a claim in tort in respect of assault, battery or false imprisonment, a claim in tort in respect of breach of statutory duty, and damages claims against a public authority (within the meaning of section 6 of the Human Rights Act 1998) for breach of Convention rights (as defined in that Act) to the extent the claim is made in reliance on section 7 of that Act. *Sub-paragraph (2)(b)* applies the exclusion in Part 3.

829.   *Sub-paragraph (3)* sets out a specific exclusion for services in relation to clinical negligence. *Sub-paragraph (4)* excludes services provided in relation to a matter arising under a family enactment (as defined in paragraph 12 of Part 1 of Schedule 1).

Paragraph 4: Working with children and vulnerable adults

830.   *Sub-paragraph (1)(a)* brings within the scope of civil legal aid services provided in relation to the inclusion or removal of an individual from a barred list under section 2 of the Safeguarding Vulnerable Groups Act 2006. A person included in the list under section 2 is barred from regulated activity relating to children and adults. Also within the scope of civil legal aid are services provided in relation to the inclusion or removal of an individual from the lists maintained under section 81 of the Care Standards Act 2000 (individuals considered unsuitable to work with children) and section 1 of the Protection of Children Act 1999 (individuals considered unsuitable to work with vulnerable adults).

831.   *Sub-paragraph (1)(b)* brings within scope services provided in relation to a disqualification order imposed under sections 28, 29 or 29A of the Criminal Justice and Court Services Act 2000, the effect of which is to bar the person against whom the order was made from working with children.

832.   *Sub-paragraph (1)(c)* brings within scope services in relation to a direction under section 142 of the Education Act 2002, which prohibits an individual from teaching and related activities.

833.   *Sub-paragraph (2)* applies the exclusions in Part 2 and Part 3. Under paragraphs 14 and 15 of Part 3, advocacy available includes advocacy in proceedings in the First–tier Tribunal and appeals to the Upper Tribunal under the provisions listed in paragraph 14 of Part 3 concerning appeals and other applications relating to the above lists, orders and directions.

Paragraph 5: Mental health and mental capacity

834.   *Sub-paragraph (1)(a)* provides that civil legal services may be made available in relation to matters arising under the Mental Health Act 1983. These include civil procedures under which individuals may be detained in hospital for assessment or treatment for a mental disorder.

835.   *Sub-paragraph (1)(b)* provides that legal aid may be made available for applications by a prisoner to a Mental Health Review Tribunal under paragraph 5(2) of the Schedule to the Repatriation of Prisoners Act 1984.

836.   *Sub-paragraph (1)(c)* provides that civil legal services may be made available in relation to matters arising under the Mental Capacity Act 2005. Such services may relate to decisions of the Court of Protection made under that Act concerning the property, financial affairs and personal welfare of persons who lack capacity to take those decisions for themselves.

837.   *Sub-paragraph (2)* specifies that paragraph 5(1) is subject to the exclusions in Part 2 and Part 3. Advocacy available under Part 3 includes advocacy in proceedings in the First-tier Tribunal (Mental Health) and the Mental Health Review Tribunal for Wales and in appeals to the Upper Tribunal arising out of such proceedings (see paragraphs 9, 10 and 15 of Part 3). Advocacy may be made available for the purposes of proceedings in the Court of Protection to the extent that they concern certain vital interests of the individual concerned, for example, the right to life, liberty or physical safety (see paragraph 4 of Part 3 of Schedule 1).

838.   *Paragraph 5(3)* excludes services provided in relation to the creation of lasting powers of attorney or the making of advance decisions under the Mental Capacity Act 2005, but *sub-paragraph (4)* states that this does not exclude services relating to the validity, meaning, effect or applicability of a lasting power of attorney that has been created, or an advance decision that has been made.

Paragraph 6: Community care

839.   Paragraph 6 describes civil legal services provided in relation to community care services. This would include, for example, services provided in order to assist a person to obtain or challenge an assessment for adequate services, to challenge care home closures or to contest a person's involuntary removal from a home by a local authority.

840.   *Sub-paragraph (3)* defines community care services as services which a relevant person may provide under a number of listed enactments. The definition of "relevant person" allows other relevant persons to be prescribed.

Paragraph 8: Appeals relating to welfare benefits

841.	*Paragraph 8* brings within scope civil legal services in relation to a welfare benefits appeal on a point of law in the Upper Tribunal (including seeking permission from the Upper Tribunal to bring a substantive appeal), the Court of Appeal and the Supreme Court. Advocacy before the Court of Appeal and Supreme Court for these cases is in scope by virtue of paragraphs 1 and 2 of Part 3 of Schedule 1.

842.	The paragraph covers appeals on a point of law relating to a benefit, allowance, payment, credit or pension under social security enactments listed at *sub-paragraph 7(3)*, as well as the Vaccine Damage Payments Act 1979 and Part 4 of the Child Maintenance and Other Payments Act 2008. The latter two enactments have been included because appeals concerning vaccine damage payments and payments in relation to diffuse mesothelioma are currently treated as part of the welfare benefits category for the purposes of civil legal aid.

843.	*Sub-paragraph (2)* applies the exclusions in Part 2, except for paragraphs 1 and 15. These relate to personal injury and death and civil legal services in relation to a benefit, allowance, payment, credit or pension under certain enactments. *Sub-paragraph (2)(b)* applies the exclusion in Part 3 of Schedule 1.

Paragraph 7: Facilities for disabled persons
844.	*Paragraph 7* provides that civil legal services may be made available in relation to Part 1 of the Housing Grants, Construction and Regeneration Act 1996, under which local authority grants may be provided to disabled persons to help them to adapt their homes to help them to live independently.

Paragraph 9: Inherent jurisdiction of High Court in relation to children and vulnerable adults

845.	*Paragraph 9* provides that civil legal services may be made available in relation to the inherent jurisdiction of the High Court in relation to children and vulnerable adults. The High Court may exercise its inherent jurisdiction to protect children and vulnerable adults in cases that call for judicial intervention but which fall outside the relevant statutory framework. So, for example, an application for a wardship order or for an injunction to protect a person under the inherent jurisdiction of the court will be in scope.

Paragraph 10: Unlawful removal of children

846.	*Paragraph 10(1)* brings within the scope of civil legal aid services provided for an individual in relation to any of a list of specified orders and requirements where the individual is seeking to prevent the unlawful removal from the United Kingdom of a child to whom the individual is related. It also provides that civil legal services may be made available to an individual who is seeking the return of a related child who has been unlawfully removed to a place within the United Kingdom.

847.   A typical situation would be where a child resides with one parent pursuant to a residence order and there are settled arrangements for staying contact with the 'non-resident' parent, the child is collected by the 'non-resident' parent but is not returned and there is concern they may remove the child from the United Kingdom. Legal aid may be made available for the resident parent in relation to the orders or requirements to prevent the removal which are listed in sub-paragraph (1)(a) to (c). A similar situation within the UK would be where the non-resident parent does not return the child to the resident parent after a period of otherwise agreed contact has ended.

848.   *Paragraph 10(2)* brings within the scope of civil legal aid certain services provided to an individual seeking to secure the return of a related child who has been unlawfully removed to a place in the United Kingdom

849.   *Sub-paragraph (3)* applies to this category the exclusions in Parts 2 and 3 of the Schedule. *Sub-paragraph (4)* provides that a child is "related" to an individual if the individual is the child's parent or otherwise has parental responsibility for the child (for example, by way of a residence order). *Sub-paragraph (5)* defines a child as a person under 18, which is in line with the Children Act 1989 although only in exceptional cases would fresh orders be made, or orders varied, for those aged between 16 and 18.

Paragraph 11: Family homes and domestic violence

850.   *Paragraph 11* refers to civil legal services for cases where a person is seeking protection from domestic violence.

851.   *Sub-paragraphs (1) and (2)* list the types of cases that are to be within scope. They cover cases where a person is seeking a civil remedy specifically to provide protection from domestic violence, in the form of an order under Part 4 of the Family Law Act 1996 (sub-paragraph (1)) or an injunction following assault, battery or false imprisonment or an injunction or other order under the inherent jurisdiction of the High Court (sub-paragraph (2)).

852.   *Sub-paragraph (3)* applies the exclusions in Parts 2 and 3 of the Schedule to the services in scope under this paragraph, except for the exclusions for services provided in relation to assault, battery or false imprisonment and in relation to trust law.

853.   *Sub-paragraph (4)* defines "family relationship" for the purpose of this paragraph: the definition is a broad one, based on the definition of "associated persons" in the Family Law Act 1996. *Sub-paragraph (5)* gives the Lord Chancellor a power to set out in regulations when circumstances arise out of a family relationship.

Paragraph 12: Victims of domestic violence and family matters

854.   *Paragraph 12* refers to civil legal aid for victims of domestic violence in private law family cases arising out of the abusive family relationship. Only services in relation to those private law family matters will be in scope and not services for a claim in tort. For example, financial disputes or disputes about children arising from the

breakdown of an abusive relationship will be in scope for victims of domestic violence, but a claim by the victim against the abuser for damages will not.

855. *Sub-paragraph (2)* applies the general exclusions in Part 2 of the Schedule to the services in scope under this paragraph, except for the exclusion for services provided in relation to trust law. *Sub-paragraph (4)* provides that the services in scope under this paragraph will include conveyancing, but only where conveyancing will give effect to a court order made in proceedings for which legal aid has been provided under Part 1 of the Bill. This means that, in these limited circumstances, the general exclusion for conveyancing set out in Part 2 of the Schedule does not apply. *Sub-paragraph (5)* applies the general exclusion in Part 3 of the Schedule.

856. *Sub-paragraph (6)* applies a specific exclusion which removes from scope under this paragraph services provided in relation to claim in tort in respect of the abuse referred to in sub-paragraph (1).

857. *Sub-paragraph (7)* defines "family relationship" for the purpose of this paragraph in the same broad way as paragraph 11(4). *Sub-paragraph (8)* provides that cases arising out of a family relationship include matters arising under a family enactment ("family enactment" for this purpose being any of those listed in sub-paragraph (9)) and gives the Lord Chancellor a power to set out in regulations when matters otherwise arise out of a family relationship. *Sub-paragraph (9)*, in addition to providing the list of family enactments, defines "domestic violence" (covering psychological, physical and emotional abuse) and defines "adult" and "child" as a persons aged 18 or over and under 18 respectively.

858. It is intended that the regulations made under section 11 will be used to ensure that funding under this paragraph is limited to cases where there is appropriately clear evidence of the need for protection. The circumstances that will be accepted as evidence have been described by the Government in Parliament[17].

Paragraph 13: Protection of children and family matters

859. *Paragraph 13* refers to civil legal services where a person is seeking in a private law family case to protect a child from abuse by applying for any of the list of orders and procedures set out in *sub-paragraph (1)*. So, for example, civil legal aid may be made available to a person who is seeking an order under section 8 of the Children Act 1989 to prevent a person who has abused a child from having contact with that child.

860. *Sub-paragraph (2)* applies the exclusions in Parts 2 and 3 of the Schedule to the services in scope under this paragraph. *Sub-paragraph (3)* defines "abuse", "adult" and "child".

---

[17] *Hansard*, 17 April 2012, Column 222 -
http://www.publications.parliament.uk/pa/cm201212/cmhansrd/cm120417/debtext/120417-0002.htm#12041733000002

861.   It is intended that the regulations made under section 11 will be used to ensure that funding for services described in this paragraph is limited to cases where there is appropriately clear evidence of the need for protection in a similar way to those services described in paragraph 12.

Paragraph 14: Mediation in family disputes

862.   *Paragraph 14* refers to civil legal aid for mediation in relation to family disputes.

863.   Under *paragraph 14(1) and (2)* legal aid will be in scope both for mediation and for civil legal services provided in connection with the mediation. It is intended that the regulations made under section 11 will be used to determine what legal services in connection with mediation will be provided as part of legal aid. The type of legal advice to be available is described in the response to the consultation paper *Proposals for the Reform of Legal Aid in England and Wales.*

864.   *Sub-paragraph (3)* applies the exclusions in Parts 2 and 3 of the Schedule to the services in scope under this paragraph, except for the exclusions for services provided in relation to trust law. *Sub-paragraph (5)* provides that the services in scope under this paragraph will include conveyancing, where conveyancing is used to give effect to arrangements made in order to resolve a family dispute in relation to which legal aid for services described in paragraph 14 has been provided under Part 1 of the Bill. This means that, in these circumstances, the general exclusion for conveyancing, set out in Part 2 of the Schedule, does not apply.

865.   *Sub-paragraph (7)* defines "family dispute" and "family relationship" for the purposes of this paragraph ("family relationship" having the same broad meaning as in paragraph 11). *Sub-paragraph (8)* provides that cases arising out of a family relationship includes matters arising under a family enactment ("family enactment" having by virtue of *sub-paragraph (9)* the same meaning as in paragraph 12), and gives the Lord Chancellor a power to set out in regulations when matters otherwise arise out of a family relationship.

Paragraph 15: Children who are parties to family proceedings

866.   *Paragraph 15* refers to civil legal services for children in relation to family proceedings. *Sub-paragraph (1)(a) to (c)* lists the types of instances when civil legal aid may be provided, for example where the child is, or proposes to be the applicant or respondent to the proceedings, or when the child is made a party to proceedings by the court under Rule 16.2 of the Family Procedure Rules 2010.

867.   *Sub-paragraph (3)(a)* defines proceedings as family proceedings if they arise out of a family relationship, and *sub-paragraph (3)(b) and (c)* defines "family relationship" (giving it the same broad meaning as in paragraph 11) for the purpose of this paragraph. *Sub-paragraph (4)* provides that cases arising out of a family relationship include proceedings arising under a family enactment ("family enactment" having by virtue of *sub-paragraph (5)* the same meaning as in paragraph 12), and gives the Lord Chancellor a power to set out in regulations when matters arise out of a family relationship.

868.　*Sub-paragraph (5)* defines a "child" as a person under the age of 18.

Paragraph 16: Forced marriage

869.　*Paragraph 16* refers to civil legal services in relation to forced marriage protection orders, which are made under Part 4A of the Family Law Act 1996. In conjunction with paragraph 11 of the Schedule, this paragraph ensures that cases where an injunction or other order is sought to protect an individual from forced marriage or domestic violence will be within the scope of civil legal aid.

Paragraph 17: EU and International agreements concerning children

870.　*Paragraph 17* refers to civil legal services in relation to private family law matters arising under international agreements. Cases are within scope for civil legal aid if following an application being made to the Lord Chancellor under the 1980 European Convention on Child Custody or the 1980 Hague Convention, or upon an application being made for recognition and enforcement under the relevant provisions of the 2003 Brussels Regulation, court proceedings are necessary.

871.　*Paragraph 17(1)(a)* refers to civil legal services in relation to cases where an EU court decision relating to the custody of a child is to be recognised and enforced within England and Wales.

872.　*Paragraph 17(1)(b)* refers to civil legal services in relation to an application made to the Lord Chancellor under the 1980 Hague Convention in an "incoming" case in relation to a child who is or is believed to be in England and Wales. This works on the principle of returning children who have been wrongfully removed or retained to their country of habitual residence so that any issue relating to the child's custody can be determined by the courts of the country of habitual residence.

873.　*Paragraph 17(1)(c)* refers to civil legal services in relation to the recognition and enforcement of judgments in matrimonial matters and the matters of parental responsibility under the 2003 Brussels Regulation (known as "Brussels IIa"). These are cases about the recognition and enforcement in a court in England and Wales of a judgment made in a Member State. The judgments concern, for example, rights of access to children, the return of a child and practical arrangements for the exercise of rights of access.

874.　*Paragraph 17(3)* provides full definitions of the Conventions and Regulation referenced in this paragraph and *sub-paragraph (4)* makes provision about when an application is "made to the Lord Chancellor" for the purposes of this paragraph.

Paragraph 18: EU and international agreements concerning maintenance

875.　*Paragraph 18* refers to civil legal services in relation to cases where a person is applying to the courts in England and Wales to recognise or enforce a maintenance order from outside the jurisdiction, or, in the case of the EU Maintenance Regulation, is applying from outside the jurisdiction to establish within the jurisdiction a liability to pay maintenance. This would include issues of child maintenance and a former spouse's maintenance where an order was made outside England and Wales but the person liable to pay the maintenance resides in England or Wales. *Paragraph 18(1)* lists the EU Conventions and Regulation under which applications for recognition and enforcement may be made, with the exception of the EU Maintenance Regulation, in relation to which provision is made by *sub-paragraphs (2) and (3)*.

876.   *Paragraph 18(2)* refers to civil legal services provided in relation to the establishment and enforcement of maintenance orders and other decisions on maintenance across EU borders under the EU Maintenance Regulation, where the application is made under Article 56. For example, cases will be in scope where a person within the EU but outside England and Wales applies through his or her home Central Authority[18], which transmits the application to the appropriate Central Authority in the United Kingdom, for a maintenance decision made in their county of residence to be recognised and enforced through the courts in England and Wales.

877.   *Paragraph 18(3)* refers to civil legal aid for recognition, enforceability and enforcement of maintenance decisions in England and Wales where an individual has received legal aid or exemptions from costs or expenses in their Member State of origin. In such a case it is not necessary for the application to have been made via the Central Authority for it to be in scope.

878.   *Paragraph 18(4)* applies the exclusions in Parts 2 and 3 of the Schedule to the services in scope under this paragraph, except for the exclusion for services provided in relation to trust law (since in a limited number of cases, matters of trust law may arise in establishing or enforcing a liability).

879.   *Paragraph 18(5)* provides full definitions of the Conventions and Regulations referenced in this paragraph.

Paragraph 19: Judicial review

880.   *Sub-paragraph (1)* brings within the scope of civil legal aid services provided in relation to judicial review. *Sub-paragraph (2)(a)* applies the exclusions in Part 2 with the exception of personal injury or death, a claim in tort in respect of negligence, a claim in tort in respect of assault, battery or false imprisonment, a claim in tort in respect of trespass to goods, a claim in tort in respect of trespass to land, damage to property, a claim in tort in respect of breach of statutory duty, a claim for damages in respect of a breach of Convention rights where the claim is made in reliance on section 7 of the Human Rights Act 1998, civil legal services in relation to a benefit, allowance, payment, credit or pension under certain enactments, and compensation under the Criminal Injuries Compensation Scheme. *Sub-paragraph (2)(b)* also applies the exclusion in Part 3. Judicial review for the purposes of this paragraph includes any procedure in which a court, tribunal or other person mentioned in Part 3 of Schedule 1 is required by an enactment to make a decision applying the principles that are applied by the court on an application for judicial review (see the definition of

---

[18] The EU Maintenance Regulation requires each Member State to have a Central Authority for the transmission of applications in relation to maintenance obligations between Member States.

"judicial review" in *sub-paragraph (10)*). Applications for bail in connection with an application for judicial review are in scope by virtue of paragraph 5(1)(a) of Part 4 of Schedule 1.

881. *Sub-paragraph (3)* excludes services that may be provided in relation to judicial review that do not have the potential to produce real benefits for the applicant, for the applicant's family or for the environment. This means that civil legal aid may not be made available for representative actions by way of judicial review. However, *sub-paragraph (4)* ensures that if services have been provided in relation to a judicial review then those services do not cease to be available if subsequently the judicial review ceases to have the potential to produce the benefit referred to in sub-paragraph (3).

882. Subject to *sub-paragraphs (7) and (8)*, *sub-paragraph (5)* excludes services provided in relation to judicial review relating to immigration (including issues relating to rights described in paragraph 30 of Part 1 of this Schedule (immigration: rights to enter and remain)) where the same or substantially the same issues have already been the subject of judicial review or an appeal to a tribunal or court within a period of 1 year, starting on the day the previous judicial review or appeal was determined and the prior judicial review or appeal was not determined in the applicant's or appellant's favour or by a decision by the UKBA to withdraw its decision.

883. Subject to *sub-paragraphs (7) and (8)*, *sub-paragraph (6)* excludes services provided in relation to judicial review of removal directions, where the directions were given not more than a year after the later of the decision to remove the individual from the United Kingdom by way of removal directions, the refusal of leave to appeal against such a decision or the determination or withdrawal of an appeal against such a decision.

884. *Sub-paragraph (7)* provides that *sub-paragraphs (5) and (6)* do not exclude services provided to an individual in relation to judicial review of a negative decision in relation to an asylum application (within the meaning of the Council Directive 2005/85/EC of 1 December 2005 on minimum standards on procedures in Member States for granting and withdrawing refugee status) where there is no right of appeal to the First-tier Tribunal against the decision or in relation to judicial review of a certificate issued under section 94 or 96 of the Nationality, Immigration and Asylum Act 2002. Section 94 allows the Secretary of State to issue a certificate on a number of different grounds, such as that an asylum claim is clearly unfounded, and the certificate prevents an appeal to the First-tier Tribunal being brought while an individual is in the United Kingdom. Section 96 allows the Secretary of State to issue a certificate preventing an appeal to the First-tier Tribunal on an issue where a person has already had an opportunity to raise the issue in an earlier appeal.

885. *Sub-paragraph (8)* provides that the exclusions at *sub-paragraphs (5) and (6)* do not prevent civil legal services from being provided in relation to judicial review of removal directions in prescribed circumstances. These circumstances would be prescribed in regulations and must relate to the period of notice given of removal and/or the reasons for proposing that period.

Paragraph 20: Habeas corpus

886. *Sub-paragraph (1)* brings within the scope of civil legal aid services in relation to an application for a writ of habeas corpus, a common law remedy enabling an individual to challenge the legality of the individual's detention. *Sub-paragraph (2)* applies the exclusions in Parts 2 and 3. Applications for bail in connection with an application for habeas corpus are in scope by virtue of paragraph 5(1)(a) of Part 4 of Schedule 1.

Paragraph 21: Abuse of position or powers by public authority

887. *Sub-paragraph (1)* brings within the scope of civil legal aid services in relation to a claim against a public authority for its abuse of position or power. This is in addition to any claim for judicial review or habeas corpus.

888. *Sub-paragraph (2)(a)* applies the exclusions in Part 2 with the exception of those relating to personal injury or death, a claim in tort in respect of negligence, a claim in tort in respect of assault, battery or false imprisonment, a claim in tort in respect of trespass to goods, a claim in tort in respect of trespass to land, damage to property, a claim in tort in respect of breach of statutory duty and a damages claim for breach of Convention rights by a public authority to the extent that the claim is made in reliance on section 7 of the Human Rights Act 1998. For the purposes of this paragraph, *sub-paragraph (4)* defines "public authority" as having the same meaning as in section 6 of the Human Rights Act 1998. *Sub-paragraph (2)(b)* applies the exclusion in Part 3 of Schedule 1. *Sub-paragraph (3)* excludes services provided in relation to clinical negligence.

889. *Sub-paragraph (4)* provides that, in order for an act or omission by a public authority to constitute abuse of its position or powers for the purposes of this paragraph, it must be deliberate or dishonest and result in harm to a person or property that was reasonably foreseeable.

Paragraph 22: Breach of Convention rights by public authority

890. *Sub-paragraph (1)* brings within the scope of civil legal aid services in relation to a claim in tort and other claims for damages in respect of an act or omission by a public authority which involved a significant breach of Convention rights.

891. *Sub-paragraph (2)(a)* applies the exclusions in Part 2 with the exception of those in relation to personal injury or death, a claim in tort in respect of negligence, a claim in tort in respect of assault, battery or false imprisonment, a claim in tort in respect of trespass to goods, a claim in tort in respect of trespass to land, damage to property and a claim in tort in respect of breach of statutory duty. It also provides an exception to the general exclusion in paragraph 12 of Part 2 for a damages claim for breach of Convention rights by a public authority to the extent that the claim is made in reliance on section 7 of the Human Rights Act 1998. *Sub-paragraph (2)(b)* applies the exclusion in Part 3 of Schedule 1.

892. *Sub-paragraph (3)* excludes services provided in relation to clinical negligence.

Paragraph 23: Clinical Negligence and severely disabled infants

893.   *Sub-paragraph (1)* brings within the scope of civil legal aid services for damages claims in respect of clinical negligence which has caused a neurological injury as a result of which the child is severely disabled, subject to two conditions being met.

894.   Firstly, under *sub-paragraph (2)*the negligence must have occurred while the individual was in the mother's womb or during birth or before the end of either of the following time periods: (i) where the individual is born before the beginning of the 37th week of pregnancy, eight weeks after the first day of what would have been that week; or (ii) where the individual is born during or after the 37th week of pregnancy, eight weeks after birth.

895.   The second condition is set out in *sub-paragraph (3)* and provides that the services are made available to the individual or, where the individual has died, to the individual's personal representative.

896.   *Sub-paragraph (4)* applies the exclusions in Part 2 with the exception of those relating to personal injury or death, a claim in tort in respect of negligence, a claim in tort in respect of assault, battery or false imprisonment and a claim in tort in respect of breach of statutory duty.

Paragraph 24 Special Immigration Appeals Commission

897.   *Paragraph 24* brings within the scope of civil legal aid services provided in relation to proceedings before the Special Immigration Appeals Commission.

898.   *Sub-paragraph (2)* applies the exclusions and exceptions in Parts 2 and 3 of the Schedule. Advocacy before the Commission is within scope under paragraph 21 of Part 3. Applications for bail in connection with an appeal to the Special Immigration Appeals Commission are in scope by virtue of paragraph 5(1)(a) of Part 4 of Schedule 1.

Paragraph 25 Immigration: detention

899.   *Paragraph 25* brings within the scope of civil legal aid services provided in relation to the immigration-related detention powers referred to in *sub-paragraph (1)*.

900.   *Sub-paragraph (2)* applies the exclusions and exceptions in Parts 2 and 3 of the Schedule. Applications for bail in connection with immigration-related detention are in scope by virtue of paragraph 5(1)(a) of Part 4 of Schedule 1. Advocacy in the magistrates' court in proceedings in relation to bail under Schedule 2 to the Immigration Act 1971 or arrest under Schedule 2 or 3 to that Act is in scope by virtue of paragraph 8(b) of Part 3 of Schedule 1. Advocacy may be provided for certain proceedings in the First-tier Tribunal and the Upper Tribunal under paragraphs 11 and 15 of Part 3.

Paragraph 26 Immigration: temporary admission

901.   *Paragraph 26* brings within the scope of civil legal aid services provided in relation to temporary admission to the United Kingdom under the provisions referred to in *sub-paragraph (1)*. Temporary admission is an alternative to detention under immigration powers.

902.   *Sub-paragraph (2)* applies the exclusions in Parts 2 and 3 of the Schedule. Advocacy before the First-tier Tribunal and the Upper Tribunal for these cases is in scope by virtue of paragraphs 11 and 15 of Part 3 of Schedule 1. Advocacy in the magistrates' court in relation to arrest under Schedule 2 to the Immigration Act 1971 is in scope by virtue of paragraph 8(b) of Part 3 of Schedule 1.

Paragraph 27 Immigration: residence etc restrictions

903.   *Paragraph 27* brings within the scope of civil legal aid services in relation to restrictions imposed on an individual, such as restrictions on place of residence, under the provisions referred to in *sub-paragraph (1)*. Restrictions are an alternative to detention under immigration powers.

904.   *Sub-paragraph (2)* applies the exclusions in Parts 2 and 3 of the Schedule. Advocacy before the First-tier Tribunal and the Upper Tribunal for these cases is in scope by virtue of paragraphs 11 and 15 of Part 3 of Schedule 1. Advocacy in the magistrates' court in relation to arrest under Schedule 2 to the Immigration Act 1971 is in scope by virtue of paragraph 8(b) of Part 3 of Schedule 1.

Paragraph 28 Immigration: victims of domestic violence and indefinite leave to remain

905.   *Paragraph 28(1)* brings within the scope of civil legal aid services in relation to an application for indefinite leave to remain on the grounds that an individual has been granted leave to enter or remain in the United Kingdom for a limited period as the partner of someone present or settled in the United Kingdom and the relationship has broken down permanently because the individual was the victim of domestic violence. This means that individuals applying for indefinite leave to remain in the United Kingdom under rules 289A to 289C of the Immigration Rules (indefinite leave to remain in the United Kingdom as the victim of domestic violence) will be within the scope of civil legal aid.

906.   *Sub-paragraph (2)* applies the exclusions in Parts 2 and 3 of the Schedule. Advocacy before the First-tier Tribunal and the Upper Tribunal for these cases is in scope by virtue of paragraphs 13 and 15 of Part 3 of Schedule 1. *Sub-paragraph (3)* provides a specific exclusion from this paragraph for attendance at an interview conducted on behalf of the Secretary of State with a view to reaching a decision on the application described in sub-paragraph (1).

Paragraph 29 Immigration: victims of domestic violence and residence cards

907. *Paragraph 29(1)* brings within the scope of civil legal aid services for an individual in relation to a residence card application where, amongst other things, the individual satisfies the condition in regulation 10(5)(d)(iv) of the Immigration (European Economic Area) Regulations 2006 (S.I. 2006/1003) on the ground that the individual or a family member of the individual was the victim of domestic violence while the marriage or civil partnership of the qualified person was subsisting.

908. *Sub-paragraph (2)* applies the exclusions in Parts 2 and 3 of the Schedule. Advocacy before the First-tier Tribunal and the Upper Tribunal for these cases is in scope by virtue of paragraphs 13 and 15 of Part 3 of Schedule 1. *Sub-paragraph (3)* provides a specific exclusion from this paragraph for attendance at an interview conducted on behalf of the Secretary of State with a view to reaching a decision on the application described in sub-paragraph (1).

909. *Sub-paragraph (4)* defines, for the purposes of paragraph 29, the meaning of family members, qualified person and residence card applications (amongst other things).

Paragraph 30 Immigration: rights to enter and remain

910. *Paragraph 30* brings within the scope of civil legal aid services in relation to rights to enter and to remain in the United Kingdom under the provisions referred to in *sub-paragraph (1)*. This paragraph allows legal aid to be provided for claims for asylum.

911. *Sub-paragraph (2)* applies the exclusions in Parts 2 and 3 of the Schedule. Advocacy before the First-tier Tribunal and the Upper Tribunal for these cases is in scope by virtue of paragraphs 11 and 15 of Part 3 of Schedule 1.

912. Unless regulations provide otherwise, *sub-paragraph (3)* provides a specific exclusion from this paragraph for attendance at an interview conducted by the Secretary of State with a view to reaching a decision on a claim in respect of a right to enter or remain described in sub-paragraph (1).

Paragraph 31: Immigration: accommodation for asylum seekers

913. *Sub-paragraph (1)* brings within the scope of civil legal aid services in relation to the Secretary of State's powers to provide or arrange for the provision of accommodation for asylum seekers and failed asylum seekers and their dependants under the legislation listed in that paragraph. This includes appeals to the First-tier Tribunal (Asylum Support) under section 103 of the Immigration and Asylum Act 1999 where they concern the refusal or withdrawal of accommodation support. This provision only includes civil legal services where the application or appeal concerns accommodation.

914. *Sub-paragraph (2)* applies the exclusions in Parts 2 and 3 of Schedule 1. Under Part 3 of Schedule 1, advocacy is not available for appeals before the First-tier Tribunal (Asylum Support).

Paragraph 32: Victims of trafficking in human beings

915. *Paragraph 32* brings within the scope of civil legal aid services provided to an individual who is a victim of human trafficking.

916. *Sub-paragraph (1)* brings within the scope of civil legal services provided in relation to an application by that individual for leave to enter or remain in the United Kingdom. Advocacy in relation to appeals in relation to such applications in the First-tier Tribunal and Upper Tribunal is also within scope buy virtue of paragraphs 13 and 15 of Part 3 of Schedule 1.

917. *Sub-paragraph (2)* brings within the scope of civil legal aid services provided to such an individual (or their personal representative) in relation to a claim under employment law arising in connection with the individual's exploitation.

918. *Sub-paragraph (3)* brings within the scope of civil legal aid services provided to such an individual (or their personal representative) in relation to a claim for damages arising in connection with the trafficking or exploitation of the individual.

919. *Sub-paragraph (1)* is subject to the exclusions in Parts 2 and 3 of Schedule 1.

920. *Sub-paragraph (2) and (3)* are subject to the exclusions in Part 2 of this Schedule, with the exception of personal injury or death, a claim in tort in respect of negligence, a claim in tort in respect of assault, battery or false imprisonment, a claim in tort in respect of trespass to goods, a claim in tort in respect of trespass to land, damage to property and a claim in tort in respect of breach of statutory duty. *Sub-paragraphs (2) and (3)* are subject to the exclusion in Part 3 of this Schedule.

Paragraph 33: Loss of home

921. *Paragraph 33* relates to cases where an individual is at risk of losing their home.

922. *Sub-paragraph (1)* brings within the scope of legal aid services provided to an individual in relation to court orders for sale or possession of the individual's home or eviction of the individual (or others) from the individual's home. So, for example, legal aid will be available to a person facing the potential immediate loss of their home as result of outstanding mortgage or rent arrears. Legal aid will also, for example, be available for a person who is unlawfully evicted from their home by a landlord.

923. *Sub-paragraph (2)* brings within scope services provided to an individual in relation to certain bankruptcy matters. These are services provided in relation to a bankruptcy order against an individual where that person's estate includes their home and where the bankruptcy proceedings are not brought voluntarily by the person concerned (and includes services provided in relation to a statutory demand). Such proceedings are included within the scope of civil legal aid because they can result in the loss of an individual's home.

924.　*Sub-paragraph (3)* applies the exclusions of Part 2 of Schedule 1 except in relation to business matters. *Sub-paragraph (5)* ensures that civil legal services are within the scope of civil legal aid where they relate to proceedings for sale or possession of an individual's home brought by the trustee in bankruptcy under section 14 of the Trusts and Land and Appointment of Trustees Act 1996 in reliance on section 335A of the Insolvency Act 1986. This will cover, for example, legal aid for the former spouse of a bankrupt whose home is at risk as a result of an application for sale brought by the trustee in bankruptcy.

925.　*Sub-paragraph (6)* disapplies the Part 2 exclusions relating to a claim in tort in respect of assault, battery or false imprisonment, a claim in tort in respect of trespass to goods, a claim in tort in respect of trespass to land, damage to property and a claim in tort in respect of breach of statutory duty in relation to counterclaims in possession/sale proceedings and in relation to unlawful eviction. This ensures that heads of claim in tort, commonly relied upon in possession proceedings and unlawful eviction cases, are not excluded from the scope of *paragraph 33*. This will include, for example, unlawful eviction claims brought by non-tenant occupiers

926.　*Sub-paragraph (8)* excludes certain matters that, to the extent that they are to be within the scope of civil legal aid, are covered by *paragraph 12* (victims of domestic violence and family matters).

927.　*Sub-paragraphs (9) to (13)* ensure that *paragraph 33* does not bring within scope services provided to persons who unarguably are occupying premises as a trespasser and entered the premises as such. This ensures that legal aid is not available to people who are squatting and face proceedings for eviction.

Paragraph 34: Homelessness

928.　*Paragraph 34* brings within the scope of civil legal aid services provided in relation to the provision of accommodation and assistance under Parts 6 and 7 of the Housing Act 1996 to persons who are homeless or threatened with homelessness as defined in the 1996 Act.

929.　This paragraph is subject to the exclusions in Parts 2 and 3 of Schedule 1.

Paragraph 35: Risk to health or safety in rented home

930.　*Paragraph 35* relates to housing disrepair cases where there is a serious risk to the health or safety of the individual or a family member in occupation.

931.　*Sub-paragraph (1)* brings within scope of civil legal aid services provided to a person seeking the removal or reduction of a serious risk to their (or a family member's) health and safety where the serious risk arises from a deficiency in the person's rented or leased home and the civil legal services are provided in order to ensure that the landlord acts to address the risk. Consequently, in accordance with the proposals in the response to the consultation paper *Proposals for the Reform of Legal Aid in England and Wales*, it is intended that legal aid will be available for serious disrepair cases where a person is primarily seeking to remedy the disrepair rather than claiming damages

932.   *Paragraph 35* is subject to the exclusions in Part 2 of Schedule 1, except the exclusions in respect of damage to property and a claim in tort in respect of breach of statutory duty. It is also subject to the exclusions in Part 3 of the Schedule.

Paragraph 36 Anti-social behaviour

933.   *Paragraph 36* brings within the scope of civil legal aid services provided to persons in respect of anti-social behaviour-related matters in the county court. Anti-social behaviour matters dealt with in the magistrates' court fall within the scope of criminal legal aid. *Sub-paragraph (1)* lists the relevant matters, namely orders against an individual under section 1B of the Crime and Disorder Act 1998 (county court orders relating to anti-social behaviour), related interim orders and intervention orders under sections 1D and 1G of that Act and anti-social behaviour injunctions against an individual under section 153A of the Housing Act 1996.

934.   This paragraph is subject to the exclusions in Parts 2 and 3 of Schedule 1.

Paragraph 37 Protection from harassment

935.   *Sub-paragraph (1)* brings within the scope of civil legal aid services provided in relation to an injunction under section 3 or 3A of the Protection from Harassment Act 1997 and services provided in relation to the variation or discharge of a restraining order under section 5 or 5A of that Act. Sections 3 and 3A of the Protection from Harassment Act 1997 concern the making of injunctions to restrain conduct amounting to harassment. Section 5 of the Protection from Harassment Act 1997 enables a court on sentencing or dealing with a defendant on conviction to make a restraining order to protect a victim or other person from harassment or fear of violence. Section 5A allows a court on acquittal to make a restraining order to protect a person from harassment. Services provided in relation to sections 5 and 5A are within scope only as regards an application to vary or discharge the restraining order made under those provisions, for example where a victim may feel that they may be at risk of danger or harassment from an ex-partner.

936.   *Sub-paragraph (2)* applies the exclusions in Parts 2 and 3 of Schedule 1. Advocacy that may be made available under Part 3 includes advocacy in the Crown Court and a magistrates' court in relation to an application to vary or discharge a restraining order made under section 5 or 5A of the Protection from Harassment Act 1997 (see, respectively, paragraph 6(a) and paragraph 8(c) of Part 3 of Schedule 1). Injunctions under sections 3 and 3A of the Protection from Harassment Act 1997 are made by the High Court or a county court and, under paragraphs 3 and 5 of Part 3 of Schedule 1, advocacy may be available for such proceedings.

Paragraph 38: Gang-related violence

937.   *Sub-paragraph (1)* brings within the scope of civil legal aid services provided in relation to injunctions under Part 4 of the Policing and Crime Act 2009.   Under Part 4 of that Act, a court may make an injunction if it is satisfied to the civil standard of proof that the respondent has engaged in, encouraged or assisted gang-related violence and if it considers it necessary for an injunction to be granted to prevent the respondent from engaging in, encouraging or assisting gang-related violence and/or to protect the respondent from gang-related violence.

938.   *Sub-paragraph (2)* applies the exclusions in Parts 2 and 3 of Schedule 1. Applications under Part 4 of the Policing and Crime Act 2009 are made to the High Court or a county court so, under paragraphs 3 and 5 of Part 3 of Schedule 1, advocacy may be available.

Paragraph 39: Sexual offences

939.   *Sub-paragraph (1)* brings within the scope of civil legal aid services provided in relation to a sexual offence, but only where the services are provided to the victim of the offence or, where the victim has died, to the victim's personal representative. This, for example, allows legal aid to be made available for a civil claim against the alleged perpetrator of an offence or against a person that negligently failed to prevent a sexual offence.

940.   *Sub-paragraph (2)(a)* applies the exclusions in Part 2 of Schedule 1 except for those in relation to personal injury or death, a claim in tort in respect of negligence, a claim in tort in respect of assault, battery or false imprisonment, a claim in tort in respect of breach of statutory duty and a damages claim for breach of Convention rights by a public authority to the extent that the claim is made in reliance on section 7 of the Human Rights Act 1998. *Sub-paragraph (2)(b)* applies the exclusion in Part 3.

941.   *Sub paragraph (4)* ensures that civil legal services are capable of being provided in relation to incitement to commit a sexual offence, encouraging or assisting a sexual offence which the person intended or believed would be committed, conspiracy to commit a sexual offence, and an attempt to commit a sexual offence.   *Sub-paragraph (5)* ensures that civil legal services are capable of being provided in relation to conduct which would be a sexual offence under the Sexual Offences Act 2003 or under section 1 of the Protection of Children Act 1978 but for the fact the conduct occurred before those provisions were in force. *Sub-paragraph (6)* ensures that conduct falls within the definition of a sexual offence for the purposes of paragraph 39 whether or not there have been criminal proceedings in relation to the conduct and whatever the outcome of any such proceedings.

Paragraph 40: Proceeds of crime

942.   *Sub-paragraph (1)* brings within the scope of civil legal aid services provided to an individual in relation to the confiscation proceedings under the Proceeds of Crime Act 2002 listed in that sub-paragraph. These include, for example, proceedings in relation to the discharge or variation of a disclosure order.

943.   *Sub-paragraph (2)* applies the exclusions in Part 2 of Schedule 1, except in relation to business matters. Sub-paragraph (2) also applies the exclusion in Part 3 in relation to advocacy. Under paragraphs 6(b) and 8(d) of Part 3 advocacy may be made available for the purposes of proceedings in the Crown Court and a magistrates' court in relation to any of the proceedings under the Proceeds of Crime Act 2002 referred to in paragraph 40(1).

944.   *Sub-paragraph (3)* excludes from the scope of civil legal aid services provided for a defendant in relation to directions under section 54(3) of the Proceeds of Crime Act 2002 about distribution of funds in the hands of a receiver or directions under section 67D of that Act about distribution of proceeds of realisation. This is because these directions relate to the application of sums at the end of the confiscation enforcement process and the procedure is primarily intended to enable third parties to have their last opportunity to claim that money or property as theirs.

945.   *Sub-paragraph (4)* provides that where a confiscation order has been made against a defendant under Part 2 of the Proceeds of Crime Act 2002 and varied under section 29 of that Act (which allows for variation of confiscation orders made at a time when the defendant had absconded), services for the defendant in relation to any subsequent application for compensation under section 73 of that Act are excluded from scope.

Paragraph 41: Inquests

946.   *Sub-paragraph (1)* brings within the scope of civil legal aid services provided for an individual in relation to an inquest into the death of a member of the individual's family.

947.   *Sub-paragraph (2)* applies the exclusions in Part 2 of Schedule 1, except in relation to personal injury or death, and applies the exclusion in Part 3.

948.   *Sub-paragraph (3)* explains when an individual is a member of another individual's family for the purposes of this paragraph.

Paragraph 42: Environmental pollution

949.   *Paragraph 42* refers to civil legal services provided in relation to injunctions for nuisance arising from environmental pollution. *Sub-paragraph (1)* allows the Lord Chancellor to prescribe the types of pollution of the environment that will be covered. The power may be used, for example, to prescribe pollution resulting in particular types of harm.

Paragraph 43: Equality

950.   *Sub-paragraph (1)* refers to civil legal services provided in relation to a contravention of the Equality Act 2010 or a previous discrimination enactment. Such services are in scope where they relate to a freestanding cause of action under the Equality Act 2010 or previous discrimination enactments, or where an alleged contravention of the Equality Act 2010 or previous discrimination enactments arises in the course of other proceedings.

951. *Sub-paragraph (2)(a)* applies the exclusions in Part 2 of Schedule 1, except for civil legal services in relation to a benefit, allowance, payment, credit or pension under certain enactments. *Sub-paragraph (2)(b)* applies the exclusion in Part 3 of Schedule 1.

Paragraph 44: Cross-border disputes

952. *Paragraph 44(1)* refers to civil legal services provided in relation to proceedings in circumstances in which the services are required to be provided under Council Directive 2002/8/EC of 27 January 2003 to improve access to justice in cross-border disputes. The Directive sets out minimum common rules relating to legal aid in disputes where the party applying for funding is domiciled or habitually resident in a Member State other than the Member State where the court is sitting or the decision is to be enforced. Paragraph 44 is not subject to the exclusions in Part 2 or Part 3 of Schedule 1.

Paragraph 45: Terrorism prevention and investigation measures etc

953. *Paragraph 45* brings within the scope of civil legal aid services provided in relation in relation to Terrorism Prevention and Investigation Measures (TPIM) notices to an individual to whom the notice relates. TPIM notices have replaced control orders. The amendment also brings into scope civil legal services provided in relation to certain control order proceedings that were subject to savings provisions in the Terrorism Prevention and Investigation Measures Act 2011.

Paragraph 46: Connected matters

954. *Paragraph 46* confers power on the Lord Chancellor to make regulations about the circumstances in which civil legal aid may be made available for services not listed in Part 1 of Schedule 1 where they are provided in connection with the provision of services that are listed in Part 1. It may be appropriate for such services to be provided, for example, where a case raises a number of different matters, not all of which will be in scope. Regulations made under this paragraph may prescribe exceptions from the exclusions in Part 2 and Part 3 of Schedule 1 and any other prescribed exclusions.

Printed in the UK by The Stationery Office Limited under the authority and superintendence of Carol Tullo, Controller of Her Majesty's Stationery Office and Queen's Printer of Acts of Parliament

5/2012   20563   19585